THE
KING JESUS GOSPEL

THE ORIGINAL GOOD NEWS REVISITED

CONTENTS

I echo the words of C. H. Dodd:

What do we mean by preaching the Gospel?

At various times and in different circles the Gospel has been identified with this or that element in the general complex of ideas broadly called Christian; with the promise of immortality, with a particular theory of the Atonement, with the idea of "the fatherhood of God and the brotherhood of man," and so forth.

What the Gospel was, historically speaking, at the beginning, and during the New Testament period, I hope these lectures have in some measure defined. No Christian of the first century had any doubt what it was, or any doubt of its relevance to human need.[1]

And those of N. T. Wright:

I am perfectly comfortable with what people normally mean when they say "the gospel". I just don't think it is what Paul means. In other words, I am not denying that the usual meanings are things that people ought to say, to preach about, to believe. I simply wouldn't use the word "gospel" to denote those things.[2]

THE
KING JESUS GOSPEL
THE ORIGINAL GOOD NEWS REVISITED

SCOT MCKNIGHT

ZONDERVAN.com/
AUTHORTRACKER
follow your favorite authors

ZONDERVAN

The King Jesus Gospel
Copyright © 2011 by Scot McKnight

This title is also available as a Zondervan ebook. Visit www.zondervan.com/ebooks.

This title is also available in a Zondervan audio edition. Visit www.zondervan.fm.

Requests for information should be addressed to:
Zondervan, *Grand Rapids, Michigan* 49530

Library of Congress Cataloging-in-Publication Data

McKnight, Scot.
      The king Jesus gospel : revisiting the original good news/ Scot McKnight.
         p. cm.
      Includes bibliographical references.
      ISBN 978-0-310-49298-6 (hardcover)
      1. Jesus Christ — Person and offices — Biblical teaching. 2. Bible. N.T. —
Theology. 3. Evangelistic work. I. Title.
BT203.M359 2011
232'.8 — dc22   2011008893

Cover design: Rob Monacelli
Interior design: Matthew Van Zomeren

Printed in the United States of America

12 13 14 15 16 /DCI/ 22 21 20 19 18 17 16 15 14 13 12 11 10 9 8 7 6 5 4

For

Patrick Mitchel and *Irish Bible Institute*

David deSilva and *Ashland Theological Seminary*

Wes Olmstead and *Briercrest Schools*

Coenie Burger and the *University of Stellenbosch*

Gabe Lyons and the *Q Conference*

Jerry Rushford and *Pepperdine Bible Lectures*

Chuck Conniry, Terry Dawson, and *George Fox University*

David Shepherd and *Belfast Bible College* and *Queens University Belfast*

My 4010 Fourth-Year Seminar Students

Foreword by
N. T. Wright

PART OF THE GENIUS of genuine Christianity is that each generation has to think it through afresh. Precisely because (so Christians
believe) God wants every single Christian to grow up in understanding as well as trust, the Christian faith has never been something that
one generation can sort out in such a way as to leave their successors
with no work to do. Like a young man inheriting a vast fortune,
such a legacy could just make you lazy. All you'd have to do would
be to look things up in the book, or to remember how it was when
your favourite pastor used to do it, and that would be it. No room
for character. No room for full human maturity—never mind full
Christian maturity.

Some versions of Christianity are constantly trying to build up
that sort of accumulated capital, but it can't be done. The Christian
faith is kaleidoscopic, and most of us are color-blind. It is multidi-
mensional, and most of us manage to hold at most two dimensions
in our heads at any one time. It is symphonic, and we can just about
whistle one of the tunes. So we shouldn't be surprised if someone
comes along and draws our attention to other colors and patterns
that we hadn't noticed. We shouldn't be alarmed if someone sketches
a third, a fourth, or even a fifth dimension that we had overlooked.
We ought to welcome it if a musician plays new parts of the harmony
to the tune we thought we knew.

We ought, in other words, to welcome a book like this new one
from Scot McKnight. Many of us have known Scot for years as one
of the most powerful and able New Testament scholars on the Amer-

ican scene—and, in a measure, on the world scene. Scot has long ago won his spurs: he knows his texts inside out and has thought long and wrestled hard with their meaning and interpretation. What's more, Scot has maintained his cutting edge as a praying Christian, determined to serve the church, to advance the gospel, and to help others develop and deepen their spiritual life. Some professors, distancing themselves from their own past, like to sneer or poke fun at the poor benighted ignoramuses still stuck in superficial forms of faith. Not so with Scot. When he challenges traditional ways of understanding, it is because he has spent quality time with the Bible and the Christian tradition, and he is in a strong position to tell us where we've been telling only half the story or getting the picture out of kilter.

The revolution Scot is proposing is massive—so massive that I doubt whether any of his colleagues, and certainly not this writer, will at once agree with every detail. We will all want to nuance some things differently, to highlight other points, or to emphasise other angles. That is to be expected. But the large thesis that is advanced here, in parallel with other similar cases that some of us are trying to make, is that the movement that has long called itself "evangelical" is in fact better labeled "soterian." That is, we have thought we were talking about "the gospel" when in fact we were concentrating on "salvation."

Well, you say, but isn't the gospel about salvation? Yes and no, replies Scot (quite rightly). Why, after all, did the early Christians call Matthew, Mark, Luke, and John "the gospel" (not "the gospels": one gospel, four telling, was how they saw it)? Answer—according to Scot, and I am convinced he's right: "the gospel" is the story of Jesus of Nazareth told as the climax of the long story of Israel, which in turn is the story of how the one true God is rescuing the world. Suddenly the Gospels and Acts, for so long regarded simply as "the back story" as opposed to "the gospel," come into their own. I won't spoil your reading of this book by explaining how it works out; suffice it to say that there are plenty of new colors and patterns, plenty of new dimensions, and some fresh tunes (well, new to most of us, anyway) as well as new and rich harmonies.

Scot McKnight has his finger on a sore spot in contemporary Christianity, particularly in America. For many people, "the gospel" has shrunk right down to a statement about Jesus' death and its meaning, and a prayer with which people accept it. That matters, the way the rotor blades of a helicopter matter. You won't get off the ground without them. But rotor blades alone don't make a helicopter. And a microcosmic theory of atonement and faith don't, by themselves, make up "the gospel."

Once, long ago, I heard John Stott say that some people had been talking about "the irreducible minimum gospel." He dismissed such an idea. "Who wants an irreducible minimum gospel?" he asked. "I want the full, biblical gospel." Well, hold onto your seats. That's what Scot McKnight is giving you in this book. As I said, everyone will find something to disagree with here and there. But we all urgently need to allow this deeply biblical vision of "the gospel" to challenge the less-than-completely-biblical visions we have cherished for too long, around which we have built a good deal of church life and practice. This book could be one of God's ways of reminding the new generation of Christians that it has to grow up to take responsibility for thinking things through afresh, to look back to the large world of the full first-century gospel in order then to look out on the equally large world of twenty-first-century gospel opportunity.

N. T. Wright, University of St Andrews
(Research Professor of New Testament and Early Christianity; formerly Bishop of Durham)

FOREWORD BY
DALLAS WILLARD

AT THE ROOT OF THE MANY PROBLEMS that trouble the "church visible" today, there is one simple source: the message that is preached. Note first of all that there is today no one message that is heard, but three or four prominent ones. And these oppose and overlap one another in various ways. For the outside onlooker as well as the devoted church member, it is a scene of confusion, which can elicit no firm and coherent response of the whole person from their whole life, or of church groups attempting genuinely and effectively to serve Christ in the contemporary world. Second, because of that confusion, what is ordinarily heard as the message given does not lead the hearer who tries to respond into a life of *discipleship* to Jesus Christ. Accordingly, the personal and social transformation that is so clearly anticipated in the biblical writers and is so clearly present in the acknowledged "great ones" of The Way rarely becomes real. Only a life of intelligent discipleship could bring it to pass. Without that we have massive nominal, non-disciple "Christianity."

This leads one to ask, "What was the message that shocked the ancient world into its response to Christ and his apostles?" And what message has, on numerous subsequent occasions, pulled individuals into a life clearly "not of this world," and even shaped significant human groups in the character and power of Christ? Can we identify it and teach and live it today?

The answer to this question is "Yes!" We can today teach what Jesus taught in the manner he taught it, and that is certainly what he commissioned his disciples to do down through the ages. It is what, with his presence among them, enabled them to carry out his commission with great effect. The result has been that those who enter into the life he is now living on earth will, as the apostle Paul put it, "shine ... like stars in the sky as you hold firmly to the word of life" (Phil. 2:15). If we are going to talk about reaching the world for Christ today, nothing else will do.

Scot McKnight here presents, with great force and clarity, the one gospel of the Bible and of Jesus the King and Savior. He works from a basis of profound biblical understanding and of insight into history and into the contemporary misunderstandings that produce gospels that do not naturally produce *disciples*, but only *consumers* of religious goods and services. In the course of this he deals with the primary barrier to the power of Jesus' gospel today—that is, a view of salvation and of grace that has no connection with discipleship and spiritual transformation. It is a view of grace and salvation that, supposedly, gets one ready to die, but leaves them unprepared to live now in the grace and power of resurrection life.

The gospel of King Jesus and of his kingdom-now is indeed "the power of God that brings salvation/deliverance." To prove this, just preach, teach, and manifest the good news of life now, for you and everyone, in the kingdom of the heavens with Jesus—your whole life. Study the Gospels to see how Jesus did it, and then do it in the manner he did it. You don't need a program, a budget, or any special qualifications to do this. Just understand it in the biblical form and do it. Scot McKnight gives you the key.

> Dallas Willard is a professor at the University of Southern California's School of Philosophy. He is author of *The Divine Conspiracy* and *The Spirit of the Disciplines*.

1971

IT WAS 1971. I was a seventeen-year-old high school senior fresh into a brand new experience of faith. I was also full of zeal for evangelism but clueless about how to evangelize other than just telling my friends about what I was so passionate about—God, Jesus, the Bible, salvation, and the rapture.

My church had an evangelism program; I had attended all the sessions for Evangelism Explosion and was now paired with a leading deacon in our Baptist church for our first night of "calling" on people so we could present the gospel to them. The deacon and I knocked on the first door. Behind this door was a man whose name we had been given because he had visited our church and innocently filled out a visitor's card. The man came to the door and greeted us, but it was obvious from traces of food on his face and the napkin in his hand that he and his family were eating dinner and watching TV.

The deacon wasn't about to be deterred by such worldly issues when this man's eternity was at stake. The deacon was clever enough to work his way into the home, and there we sat for the next hour or so as the family finished dinner, cleaned the table, did the dishes, and then retired to other rooms—leaving Dad with us. My job, as a nervous newbie, was to pray and keep my mouth shut unless I had something really important to say. I did (pray) and I didn't (have anything to say). As the hour wore on, two things became apparent: first, the man wasn't at all (in my inexperienced estimation) interested in getting saved, and second, the deacon was surely convinced that the man was interested even if he had to apply every ounce of persuasion he had mastered. The deacon won, the man somehow "made a decision for Christ," we prayed with him, and then we returned to the church where everyone had gathered. When we gave our report of a salvation, everyone said, "Praise God!"

Yes, we had achieved our goal, but deep inside I was absolutely convinced the man had not made a decision for Christ. That man, too, had achieved his goal in getting us out of the house. I never saw the man at our church again, but I did recognize his face one time in our community. I wanted to apologize for our gospel presentation to him, but I had no idea how one did such a thing about what I believed to be truth.

Because of that singular event, I've looked ever since with a cynical eye at evangelistic strategies. Not because I'm not an evangelist but because I believe we are focused on the wrong thing. Most of evangelism today is obsessed with getting someone to make a *decision*; the apostles, however, were obsessed with making *disciples*. Those two words — decision and disciples — are behind this entire book. Evangelism that focuses on decisions short circuits and — yes, the word is appropriate — aborts the design of the gospel, while evangelism that aims at disciples slows down to offer the full gospel of Jesus and the apostles.

My experience has been confirmed by my students who are roughly the age I was when I began to wonder what evangelism and the gospel were about. In the first few chapters of this book, some of their observations about the gospel will appear in the sidebars. Years of discussing the gospel in my classes at North Park University have led me to two observations that have helped shape this book: first, nearly all of my Christian students tell me that the gospel they heard as they grew up primarily had to do with their sin, Jesus' death, and going to heaven. But, second, these same students tell me over and over again that they know there's something wrong with that; the gospel of Jesus wants more from us than a singular decision to get our sins wiped away so we can be safe and secure until heaven comes. The above experience with Evangelism Explosion illustrates how we can get obsessed with making a decision. If we step back enough to focus on this issue, we will see an alternate approach is far more productive.

If we step back enough to focus on the obsession with decision, we will see what has happened, what is happening, and what will

I was taught that God loved me and sent Jesus to die for my sins. I was taught the problem had already been solved. It seemed easy enough because my expected response seemed to be mostly cognitive.

So it seems this culture of people confessing Christ as Lord but not living any alternative lifestyle had set itself up to reproduce itself. I'm not sure which came first, the chicken or the egg. Either these Scripture verses [Romans 6:23; John 3:16] were seen as the gospel in its entirety, and this foundation played itself out by not having an impact in this life. Or people didn't want to live the hard life of being redeemed here and now and chose verses that set up the gospel as only concerning eternal matters.

"Darren"—a student[3]

continue to happen if we don't make some serious changes. I have heard numbers as high as 75 percent of Americans have made some kind of *decision* to accept Christ, but statistics also show that only about 25 percent of Americans go to church regularly.[4] No one would suggest that church attendance is the perfect measure of discipleship, but neither would anyone deny it is at least a baseline measure.

I recently had a conversation with David Kinnaman of the Barna Group, an organization that specializes in statistical studies of Americans and their faith. Anyone who brings up statistics about faith seems to be asking for a fight, but studies across the board—and I love to read such studies—show that the correlation between making a decision and becoming a mature follower of Jesus is not high. Here are some approximate numbers: among teenagers (ages thirteen to seventeen) almost 60 percent of the general population makes a "commitment to Jesus"—that is, they make a "decision." That number changes to just over 80 percent for Protestants and (amazingly) approaches 90 percent for nonmainline Protestants, a group that focuses more on evangelicals. As well, six out of ten Roman Catholic teens say they have made a "commitment to Jesus."

However we look at this pie, most Americans "decide" for Jesus. But if then we measure discipleship among young adults (ages eighteen to thirty-five), we find dramatic (and frankly discouraging) shifts in numbers. Barna has some measures for "discipleship," including what they call "revolutionary faith," a "biblical worldview," and "faith as a highest priority in life." Take revolutionary faith, which sorts out things like meaning in life, self-identification as a Christian, Bible reading, and prayer as well as questions about how faith has been or is transforming one's life. That almost 60 percent becomes about 6 percent, that 80 percent or so of Protestants becomes less than 20 percent, and that almost 90 percent of non-mainline Protestants becomes about 20 percent.[5]

At the most conservative of estimates, *we lose at least 50 percent of those who make decisions.* We cannot help but conclude that making a decision is not the vital element that leads to a life of discipleship. Much higher correlations can be found between routine Sunday school participation, youth group participation, and families that nurture one into faith.[6] Our focus on getting young people to make decisions—that is, "accepting Jesus into our hearts"—appears to distort spiritual formation.

I want now to say this in a stronger form: I would contend there is a minimal difference in correlation between *evangelical*[7] children and teenagers who make a decision for Christ and who later become genuine disciples, and *Roman Catholics* who are baptized as infants and who as adults become faithful and devout Catholic disciples. I am fully aware of the pointedness of this accusation, directed as it is at us who have for years contended that we are saved while Roman Catholics are (or may) not (be), but I am trying to make just that point. I'm not convinced our system works much more effectively than theirs. I am happy to be proven wrong, but being wrong here won't change the central challenges of this book.

One more point: focusing youth events, retreats, and programs on persuading people to make a decision disarms the gospel, distorts numbers, and diminishes the significance of discipleship. When I read this section of my book to some students recently, a sense of "that's so right" pervaded the room. Some of them came to faith in the heated moment of a decision-shaped, low lights, evocative music event, but also verbalized that many of their friends did too—and now they have nothing to do with following Jesus. One student said, "It makes me wonder what it is that makes faith stick."

I will return to these themes throughout this book, but for now I want to return to my story. As a result of my Evangelism Explosion experience and its aftermath in my own thinking, I developed a cynicism about evangelism. It took deep root as I continued through my college, seminary, and doctoral education. I began to pay close attention to the connection of *gospel* and *evangelism* and *salvation* and our *methods of persuasion*, which (embarrassingly at times) border on the slick and manipulative. I am convinced that there is something profoundly wrong with our evangelism and so have developed over the decades a sensitive ear for anyone with a thought about this problem.

In my earliest days of teaching at a seminary, I worked hard on incorporating "discipleship" into "evangelism" or "gospel," but I could never quite find a happy place that satisfied biblical studies and the need to evangelize. After a dozen years of seminary teaching, I shifted to a college and, lo and behold, discovered that my classes precipitated faith development toward discipleship, and even some conversions, in ways I had not anticipated. This classroom experience has led me into a quest to understand more sharply both *what the gospel is* and *what evangelism is*—and, perhaps most importantly, how to do evangelism in a way that leads beyond decisions to discipleship.

But all of this requires an answer to one big question.

CHAPTER 1

THE BIG QUESTION

THIS BOOK IS ASKING the most important—or at least one of the most important—questions we can ask today. In this book I will contend we all need to ask this question because we've wandered from the pages of the Bible into an answer that isn't biblical enough. In fact, there is both a widespread dissatisfaction with where we are and a widespread yearning for a more biblical approach to the question, and the dis-ease and yearning show up in a vigorous and invigorating discussion of this question today. One of my friends says the church is "in a fog" about this question, and another writer says there's a "fog of confusion" about it.

The question is this:

What is the gospel?

THE GOSPEL

You may be surprised. You may think the word *gospel*, a word used in the ancient world for declaring good news about something (like a wedding) but used today for our Christian message, is the one thing we *do* understand. You may think that's the one thing around which there is no fog at all. You may think the gospel is the simple thing, whereas everything else—like politics and eschatology and atonement theory and poverty—cries out for debate. Those issues need to be debated, but we really cannot debate them in a Christian manner until we get the gospel question resolved. I think we've got the gospel wrong, or at least our current understanding is only a pale reflection of the gospel of Jesus and the apostles. We need to go back to the Bible to find the original gospel.

By the time we get through digging into what the New Testament actually says, I think you will agree with me that the question noted above is the most important question we need to ask today, and I hope you will agree with me that our current answer isn't biblical enough. I'm also hopeful you will see some biblical wisdom in my proposal. I encourage you to pull out a piece of paper or open up the flyleaf of the back of this book and scribble down your answer to this most important question before you read one more word: What is the gospel?

Three Exhibits

The following three exhibits illustrate why I think we've wandered and why we are in need of going back to the Bible to ask this question all over again — as if for the first time, as if we were in Galilee listening to Jesus ourselves, or as if we were the first listeners to the apostles' gospel in some small house church in the bustling and boisterous Roman empire. In going back, I believe we will be shocked by what we find, and these three exhibits show why we will be shocked.

Exhibit A

I received an email from a reader with this question: "I know you're probably really busy. If you have time, I have a question about the gospel. I notice that the gospel writers often include in their gospel the announcement that Jesus is the Messiah. My question is, 'What is good news about the fact that Jesus is the Messiah, the descendant of David?' ... Thanks for your time!" I read that letter three times and shook my head in disbelief each time, and I did so because I wonder how we have gotten ourselves to a point where we can wonder what Jesus' being Messiah has to do with the gospel. But that emailer is not alone.

Answer A: *For this emailer, the word* gospel *was almost entirely about personal salvation. That means the gospel no longer includes the promise to Israel that Jesus was the Messiah. But let's not be hard on this emailer. Perhaps most Christians today wonder what the gospel has to do with Jesus being "Messiah."*

EXHIBIT B

John Piper, one of America's most influential pastors and authors—and deservedly so—at a big conference in April of 2010 asked this question: "Did Jesus preach Paul's gospel?" To answer it, he examined the parable of the Pharisee and the tax collector in Luke 18, where we find one of the few uses of the word *justified* in the Gospels. Then John Piper concluded that, yes, Jesus did preach Paul's gospel of justification by faith. I would defend the legitimacy of Piper's question, and I would also agree that the makings of justification by faith are indeed found in that parable of Jesus. So, it is entirely fair to ask if Jesus preached a gospel like Paul's.

But ... to begin with, there's the problem of order and even of precedence: Isn't the more important question about whether Paul preached Jesus' gospel? Moreover, there's another problem: Piper's assumption is that justification is the gospel. The Calvinist crowd in the USA—and Piper is the leading influencer in the resurgence of Calvinist thinking among evangelicals—has defined the gospel in the short formula "justification by faith." But we have to ask whether the apostles defined the gospel this way. Or, better yet, when they preached the gospel, what did they say? We will answer these questions in the pages that follow.

Answer B: *When we can find hardly any instances of our favorite theological category in the whole of the four Gospels, we need to be wary of how important our own interpretations and theological favorites are.*

EXHIBIT C

At an airport, I bumped into a pastor I recognized, and he offered a more extreme version of what we saw in Exhibit B. He asked me what I was writing, and I replied, "A book about the meaning of gospel."

"That's easy," he said, "justification by faith." After hearing that quick-and-easy answer, I decided to push further, so I asked him Piper's question: "Did Jesus preach the gospel?"

His answer made me gulp. "Nope," he said, "Jesus couldn't have.

No one understood the gospel until Paul. No one *could* understand the gospel until after the cross and resurrection and Pentecost."

"Not even Jesus?" I asked.

"Nope. Not possible," he affirmed. I wanted to add an old cheeky line I've often used: "Poor Jesus, born on the wrong side of the cross, didn't get to preach the gospel." My satire, if not sarcasm, would not have helped, so I held back. But I've heard others make similar claims about Jesus, Paul, and the gospel, and this book will offer a thorough rebuttal of this conviction.

Answer C: *For this pastor, the word* gospel *means "justification by faith," and since Jesus really didn't talk in those terms, he flat out didn't preach the gospel. Few will admit this as bluntly as that preacher did, but I'm glad some do. This view is wrong and wrongheaded.*

Harsh words, I admit.

Each of these three instances — the emailer who can't figure out how in the world "Messiah" and "gospel" are connected, and the two pastors who believe "justification by faith" and "gospel" are one and the same (one thinking Jesus preached it and the other thinking Jesus didn't and couldn't have) — illustrate my deep concern. I believe the word *gospel* has been hijacked by what we believe about "personal salvation," and the gospel itself has been reshaped to facilitate making "decisions." The result of this hijacking is that the word *gospel* no longer means in our world what it originally meant to either Jesus or the apostles.

I know this is an unusual claim, and I know some will think my claim is outlandish, so I'm going to ask you to be patient enough to hear me out. I believe we are mistaken, and that mistake is creating problems we are trying to solve. But as long as we remain mistaken, we will never solve the problems. Our system is broken and our so-called gospel broke it. We can't keep trying to improve the mechanics of the system because they're not the problem. The problem is that the system is doing what it should do because it is energized by a badly shaped gospel.

Over lunch not long ago I mentioned to a well-known American pastor what this book was about. Here is what he said to me: "Scot, we need that book. The reason we need the book is because people

A short recap of the gospel I received: Basic four spiritual law premise, justification by faith alone, plus some guilt if you didn't do the "optional" work in addition to the faith part, and a bonus of "you probably have not received that gospel" if you don't believe in a six-day creation.... Whereas the gospel I grew up with was basically "sin management," the gospel Paul is describing [in 1 Corinthians 15] is a solution to "sin" in order to "defeat" the bigger problem or enemy: "death."   *"Gary"—a student*

are confused. Not only are they confused, they don't even know they are confused."

I asked for more because he, too, seemed to observe the "fog" that others are seeing. Here's the gist of what he said: "For most American Christians, the gospel is about getting my sins forgiven so I can go to heaven when I die." Then he rolled onward: "I will never forget encountering what Dallas Willard called 'the gospel of sin management.' When I read Dallas, I knew he was right. If the gospel isn't about transformation, it isn't the gospel of the Bible. We need a book that tells us in clear terms what the gospel of the New Testament really is." That pastor is right. I hope this book helps him and others like him.

Our biggest problem is that we have an entire culture shaped by a misunderstanding of the gospel. That so-called gospel is deconstructing the church.

CHAPTER 2

GOSPEL CULTURE OR SALVATION CULTURE?

EVANGELICALISM IS A GIFT to the church and the world.

One of evangelicalism's most precious convictions, one that I hold dear, is that each person must be born again or be saved. This conviction is established on nearly every page of the Gospels, it can be found in each of the sermons in the book of Acts, and it resonates under and on the pages of the apostolic letters. Personal faith is both necessary and nonnegotiable. The gospel doesn't work for spectators; you have to participate for it to work its powers.

The widespread assumption that church bodies can baptize infants and then automatically catechize those babies into the faith when they are preteens or early teens has been challenged by evangelicalism's stubborn commitment to make a personal decision about Jesus Christ. One of my close friends, Brad Nassif, is an Eastern Orthodox theologian. He has said to me time and time again that in his tradition the people have too often been "sacramentalized" but not "evangelized." That is, they've gone through baptism and some even attend church but may not have made a personal commitment to Jesus Christ.

Theologically, Nassif believes the Orthodox Church has remained true to the gospel over the centuries and that the call to conversion resides within it. But he is also convinced that, like other historic traditions, "nominalism" has got the church by the throat. So, for Brad, the most urgent need in the Orthodox world today is the need for an aggressive internal mission of (re)converting the people, and even some clergy, to personal faith in Jesus Christ. The number of converts from the major liturgical traditions, like the Orthodox Church and the Roman Catholic Church, to evangelicalism confirms what Brad says. The sacramental process isn't enough; there must be a call for personal faith, and this has been the emphasis in evangelicalism.

Evangelicalism may be a gift to the church and world, but it's far from perfect.

Evangelicalism is known for at least two words: *gospel* and (personal) *salvation*. Behind the word *gospel* is the Greek word *euangelion* and *evangel*, from which words we get evangelicalism and evangelism. Now to our second word. Behind *salvation* is the Greek word *soteria*. I want now to make a stinging accusation. In this book I will be contending firmly that we evangelicals (as a whole) are not really "evangelical" in the sense of the apostolic gospel, but instead we are *soterians*. Here's why I say we are more soterian than evangelical: we evangelicals (mistakenly) equate the word *gospel* with the word *salvation*. Hence, we are really "salvationists." When we evangelicals see the word *gospel*, our instinct is to think (personal) "salvation." We are wired this way. But these two words don't mean the same thing, and this book will do its best to show the differences.

The irony here is obvious: the term we use to define ourselves (gospel/*euangelion*) does not define us, while the word that does define us (*soteria* or "salvation") we do not use to describe ourselves. We ought to be called *soterians* (the saved ones) instead of evangelicals. My plea is that we go back to the New Testament to discover all over again what the Jesus gospel is and that by embracing it we become true evangelicals. My prayer for this book is that it will revive a generation of evangelicals to become true evangelicals instead of just soterians. What has happened is that we have created a "salvation culture" and mistakenly assumed it is a "gospel culture."

A SALVATION CULTURE

Our emphasis on the call to personal faith has created a "salvation culture," a culture that focuses on and measures people on the basis of whether they can witness to an experience of personal salvation. Our salvation culture tends toward asking one double-barreled question: "Who is in and who is out?" Or more personally, "Are you in or out?" The evangelical culture focuses on the experience of personal salvation as the decisive factor for creating that culture. Perhaps the most important thing I can say about what this book will argue boils down to these points:

- A salvation culture and a gospel culture are not the same.
- In thinking our salvation culture is identical to a gospel culture, we betray a profound lack of awareness of what gospel means and what a gospel culture might mean for our world today.
- We are in need of going back to the Bible to discover the gospel culture all over again and making that gospel culture the center of the church.

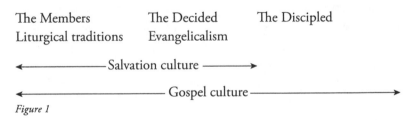

The Members   The Decided   The Discipled
Liturgical traditions   Evangelicalism

←——————— Salvation culture ———→

←———————— Gospel culture ————————→

Figure 1

Perhaps Figure 1 above will clarify matters. The big picture is this: Salvation cultures, which include but are not limited to the Roman Catholic, Orthodox, and Anglican bodies, have struggled to get The Members to become The Discipled. They will continue to struggle until they get the gospel straight and demand personal salvation. Some evangelicals are part of these liturgical traditions, but I want to simplify matters slightly, perhaps overslightly, to focus on the evangelical movement in its emphasis on personal decision. Evangelicalism, whether part of the larger liturgical traditions or separate from them, seeks to move The Members into The Decided

> At its heart, I have to say that I was raised by the
> gospel of fear.... Growing up as a child I was given
> basic ideas:
>> You're a sinner.
>> We need to be with Jesus.
>> And He saves us from hell....
> We always talked about how we are sinners and
> are drifting away from God and need to come to Him
> before He "has" to send us to Hell.
>
> *"Craig"—a student*

batch with their emphasis on personal decision and personal salvation. But evangelicals have the same struggle of moving The Decided to become the The Discipled because they have created a (sometimes smug) salvation culture in which the obsession is making the right decision so we can cross the threshold from the unsaved to the saved (The Decided). A gospel culture, though, encompasses it all and leads The Members into The Discipled because it equates the former with the latter.

Now to say this slightly more completely: all Christian traditions—and I'm thinking of all but especially the Catholic and Orthodox traditions—emphasize entrance into the church (The Members). For the more liturgically oriented traditions, entrance into the church begins with the baptism of the infant and continues into catechism. For some this is an all but automatic process: the baptized become the catechized become The Members. In class not long ago I asked one of my Roman Catholic students if he knew of any young adult who was denied "membership." His response was immediate: "Never." Making the conversion process automatic—and I'm doing my best to be dead-level honest in saying that—is disastrous for the vitality of faith and church life. This kind of gospel can deconstruct a local church, and I would finger this issue as one of the, if not *the*, origins of the demise of the church in European cultures.

This sacramental process contrasts dramatically with what happens with many Protestants, where, especially among the evangelical types, salvation occurs only if the child/youth/adult makes a (more) personal profession of faith. So the evangelical tradition wants to take a second step. That second step is to become of The Decided. In spite of the obvious and important differences here between the liturgical and evangelical traditions, each has a similar problem. Salvation cultures have struggled, are struggling, and will continue to struggle to get The Members or The Decided into the third category: The Discipled. My contention is that we have to create a gospel culture if we want The Members to be The Discipled, and it means the following example of a pastor struggling to make sense of the gospel's fullness is the paradigm we will have to deconstruct and reform.

Pastor Eric

Pastor Eric rightly knows the importance of preaching the gospel. So he begins with a clear definition, and it's a perfect expression of a salvation culture gospel: "The gospel is the good news that God offers us salvation through his Son, Jesus Christ." Eric appeals to Luke 2, where Luke writes that the angel said, "I bring you good news ... [about] a Savior ...," and then infers that the gospel is, primarily, good news about a Savior—and about the salvation he brings.

"What, then, did Christ save us from?" Eric asks next.

The answer, skipping back two Gospels, is in Matthew 1:21: "our sins."

"How?" Pastor Eric now asks. He decides that 1 Peter 3:18 gives the answer: Jesus' death and resurrection. The absence of the resurrection in most of evangelism today is appalling, so I applaud Pastor Eric's framing of the gospel here.

But then Pastor Eric makes some ominous claims that I fear will begin to unravel or at least minimize his resurrection gospel. His claims are all shaped as negatives and illustrate the heartbeat of a salvation culture's nervousness:

- The gospel is a not a call to imitate Jesus.
- It is not a public announcement that Jesus is Lord and King.
- It is not (directly) an invitation into the church.
- It does not involve a promise of the second coming.

"No," Pastor Eric continues, "these dimensions are Christian theology and true, but the gospel is the starting point. It is the good news that Jesus came to save us from our sins by dying on the cross and rising from the dead."

Pastor Eric moves on to ask, "How does one receive salvation?" His answer: by simple faith, because it is all grace. But here Pastor Eric begins to wonder about one of the most significant problems in the church: Does salvation really lead The Decided to become The Discipled? So he starts to work the words. He contends that true faith is a robust faith; it involves the mind, the heart, and the will. Frankly, he does his best to make sure salvation is by faith alone, but he wants that faith to lead (inevitably and surely) to discipleship. Yet he worries that if he presses discipleship too hard, salvation by grace and by faith alone will be compromised. And so back and forth he goes . . . and he goes back and forth because his gospel is a "salvation culture" gospel instead of a "gospel culture" gospel.

We will argue in this book that the apostolic gospel, because it was a gospel culture gospel and not a salvation culture gospel, did not have this struggle. This struggle is our own making. You can play with the words all you want, but that kind of salvation culture gospel will always create the problem of discipleship.

A salvation culture does not require The Members or The Decided to become The Discipled for salvation. Why not? Because its gospel is a gospel shaped entirely with the "in and out" issue of salvation. Because it's about making a decision. In this book we want to show that the gospel of Jesus and that of the apostles, both of which created a *gospel* culture and not simply a salvation culture, was a gospel that carried within it the power, the capacity, and the requirement to summon people who wanted to be "in" to be The Discipled. In other words, it swallowed up a salvation culture into a gospel culture.

But to create a gospel culture, we need to distinguish four categories.

CHAPTER 3

FROM STORY
TO SALVATION

You may think I'm dragging my feet by not getting straight to the meaning of the word *gospel*. We're almost there. To set the stage for defining the gospel we need to distinguish four big categories, and the themes of this book flow from these four categories:

The Story of Israel/the Bible,
The Story of Jesus,
The Plan of Salvation,
The Method of Persuasion.

A question, and I hope you take the time to think through it before you answer it: To which of these four categories would you apply the term *gospel*? Many today think the Story of Israel. The Bible's plot is the gospel itself. For some the gospel is Jesus, full stop and no discussion left. But for others, and I would put evangelicalism, Catholicism, and Orthodoxy in one way or another in this drawer, the word *gospel* aligns most naturally with the third category, the Plan of Salvation, by which I mean the (*personal*) plan of how God saves us. In fact, because of how the gospel is preached today, many also would see little difference between the Plan of Salvation and the Method of Persuasion. (More on that in a moment.)

These four categories are connected to one another and ought to build on top of one another. As can be seen in Figure 2, the foundation is the Story of Israel, upon which the Story of Jesus makes sense. The Plan of Salvation flows out of this Story of Israel/ Story of Jesus and the Method of Persuasion flows out of the Plan of Salvation.

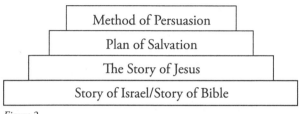

Figure 2

THE STORY OF ISRAEL

The *Story of Israel*, or the Bible, is the sweep of how the Bible's plot unfolds: the creation of the world as God's temple, the placing of two little Eikons—Adam and Eve as divine image-bearers—in the garden temple of God (called Eden) to represent God, to govern for God, and to relate to God, self, others, and the world in a redemptive way. The single task of representing God and governing God's garden was radically distorted when Adam and Eve rebelled against the good command of God. God banished them from Eden. We can't skip now to Jesus and to the New Testament and think we understand the Story of Israel/the Bible. The Bible, page after page, takes another path. There's much to say here, and since we will be revising this entire sketch in subtle but important ways later in the book, I will keep this to a minimum.

God chose one person, Abraham, and then through him one people, Israel, and then later the Church, to be God's priests and rulers in this world on God's behalf. What Adam was to do in the Garden—that is, to govern this world redemptively on God's behalf—is the mission God gives to Israel. Like Adam, Israel failed, and so did its kings. So God sent his Son to do what Adam and Israel and the kings did not (and evidently could not) do and to rescue everyone from their sins and systemic evil and Satan (the adversary). Hence, the Son is the one who rules as Messiah and Lord.

Notice this: what God does in sending the Son is to establish Jesus as the Messiah, which means King, and God established in Jesus Christ the kingdom of God, which means the King is ruling in his kingdom. We need to restate this: the idea of King and a kingdom are connected to the original creation. God wanted the Eikons, Adam and Eve, to rule in this world. They failed, so God sent his Son to rule. As its King and Messiah and Lord, the Son commissions the Church to bear witness to the world of the redemption in Jesus Christ, the true King, and to embody the kingdom as the people of God.

Finally, the Story has an aim: the consummation, when God will set it all straight as God establishes his kingdom on earth. That consummation comes with a clarification that leads us to read the whole Bible all over again: God originally placed Adam and Eve in a garden-temple, but when God gets things completely wrapped up, the garden disappears. Instead of a garden in Revelation 21–22 we find a *city*. The garden, in other words, is not the ideal condition. The ideal condition is a flourishing, vibrant, culture-creating, God-honoring, Jesus-centered city.

While this sketch of the Bible's Story may seem like an old story to many and while each line (if not word) above deserves a chapter, this is the Bible's Story, and it is more or less the Bible's only story. However, this story is not the same as the gospel. The gospel fits into this story, but it is not the story. Further, the gospel *only makes sense in that story*. Now a very important claim: *without that story there is no gospel*. This leads to a second claim: *if we ignore that story, the gospel gets distorted, and that is just what has happened in salvation cultures.*

THE STORY OF JESUS

Like talking only about *The Lion, the Witch and the Wardrobe* instead of all seven *Chronicles of Narnia*, our second category narrows to one segment of the story: the *Story of Jesus*. The Story of Jesus brings the Story of Israel to its *telos* point, to its fulfillment, to its completion, or to its resolution. I will sometimes use the word *completes* in what follows, but that word means "brings to resolution" or the Story of

Israel comes to its telos point. I do not mean to suggest the story is officially over—the church goes on and the consummation is yet to come.

The Story of Jesus is about his kingdom vision, and this kingdom vision emerges out of the creation story, out of Israel's Story of trying to live out God's design for Israel, and out of the vision of the city in the book of Revelation. One could write chapters about each of the terms and claims being made here, but we can't do that at this point because we're trying to grasp the big picture. At the center of the Story of Jesus is the narrative of his birth, his life and teachings, his miracles and actions, his death, his burial, his resurrection, and his ascension and exaltation. Inherent to the Story of Jesus are labels that define him and identify him and his role in completing Israel's Story: Messiah, Lord, Son of God, Savior, and Son of Man. The Story of Jesus as Messiah and Lord resolves what is yearning for completion in the Story of Israel. This Jesus is the one who saves Israel from its sins and the one who rescues humans from their imprisonments.

To return to my emailer: the fundamental problem the writer had in asking what Jesus as Messiah had to do with the gospel is that his understanding of the "gospel" is that it is a solution to an individual, existential, private sin-problem but not (at the same time) the resolution of a story-problem, namely, Israel's Story in search of a Messiah-solution. The Story of Jesus, though, is first and foremost a resolution of Israel's Story and because the Jesus Story completes Israel's Story, it saves. This leads to our next category.

THE PLAN OF SALVATION

Now to our third big idea: the (personal) *Plan of Salvation*. The Plan of Salvation flows out of the Story of Israel/Bible and the Story of Jesus. The Bible's Story from Israel to Jesus is the saving Story. Just as we dare not diminish the importance of this Story if we wish to grasp the gospel, so also with the saving effects of the story.

But equating the Plan of Salvation with either the Story of Israel or the Story of Jesus distorts the gospel and at times even ruins the Story. It is customary in America to refer to the "gospel plan of salvation," by which we mean *how an individual gets saved, what God has done for us, and how we are to respond if we want to be saved.* I am aware as a result of conversations with friends from other parts of the globe that "plan of salvation" may well evoke for them something closer to what I mean by "the Story of Israel and the Story of Jesus" combined. That is, for many the Plan of Salvation will evoke God's mission in this world.

With all due respect to my friends, I want to use the Plan of Salvation in a specific sense and only in that sense, and use it to refer to the saving message in particular and how we get saved. Here's the big picture: sometimes we are so singularly focused on the personal-Plan-of-Salvation and how-we-get-saved that we eliminate the Story of Israel and the Story of Jesus altogether. I recently read a book about the gospel and came away with this question: Does that author even need the Old Testament for his understanding of the gospel? Sadly, I didn't think the Old Testament even mattered. That is what happens when we equate "gospel" with the doctrines at work in the "plan of salvation." The Story of the Bible disappears, and so too does the gospel!

What then is this (personal) Plan of Salvation? By this I mean the elements or ideas that we find in the Story of the Bible that many of us, but not just evangelicals, bring together to explain how a person gets saved, gets forgiven, and gets reconciled with God, and what that person must do in order to get saved. I must confess that I'm not entirely at ease with the points I'm about to list (and not to list), as I think salvation is more robust than this. For the sake of the argument, however, these points are listed because they are more or less the way many understand the basics of personal salvation and the way many also (mis)understand the gospel itself. Here are the most common elements of the Plan of Salvation, and each of these lines warms the heart of anyone who knows God's saving power:

- God's love and grace and holiness and righteousness
- Our creation as Eikons, or image-bearers, but our choice to sin — and disobedience and original sin are involved here
- Our condition of being under God's judgment
- The good news of the atoning death of Jesus Christ that forgives us our sins and reconciles us to God

- The need for every human being to respond simply by admitting one's sinfulness, repenting from sin, and trusting in the atoning death of Jesus

It may strike you as uncommonly odd for me to make this claim, but I'm going to say it anyway: this Plan of Salvation is not the gospel. The Plan of Salvation emerges from the Story of Israel/Bible and from the Story of Jesus, but the plan and the gospel are not the same big idea. I understand this is controversial. I am denying neither salvation—or justification by faith—nor the importance of salvation in the Bible, and I believe much more could be said than what has been listed above. Still, apart from salvation we stand unreconciled before God. But what I hope to show is that the "gospel" of the New Testament cannot be reduced to the Plan of Salvation. Instead, the Plan of Salvation, as Figure 2 above illustrates, flows out of (and is founded upon) the Story of Israel and the Story of Jesus. The good news is that the more we submerge "salvation" into the larger idea "gospel," the more robust will become our understanding of salvation.

Before I move on to the fourth category, an observation that reveals the significance of making distinctions between gospel, which I will examine in the pages that follow, and the Plan of Salvation: for most of my adult life I have both heard complaints and

---

The gospel I have received...

God is real ... God loves us ... The gospel and salvation are for everyone ... God sent his Son to us, and he was crucified for us.

The way to respond to God's love is to believe in him and the reward is everlasting life.

These people [who taught me the gospel] want to explain the gospel as simply as possible ... [and they want to] focus only the "nice side" of the gospel, to let them accept the gospel simply as receiving a blessing.

"John"—a student

participated in the complaining about how to get "saved" people more active in discipleship. All sorts of motivational ploys have been attempted, and I've invented a few myself. Most of them, perhaps all, are—and now to quote a great Irish writer Frank O'Connor—"held together by pins and Hail Marys."[8]

I'm convinced there's a fundamental misperception at work in the motivational ploys. Namely, not only have we reduced the robust view of salvation to these four or five points; we are also asking the Plan of Salvation to do something it was never intended to do. The Plan of Salvation, to put this crudely, isn't discipleship or justice or obedience. The Plan of Salvation leads to one thing and to one thing only: salvation. Justification leads to a declaration by God that we are in the right, that we are in the people of God; it doesn't lead inexorably to a life of justice or goodness or loving-kindness. If it did, all Christians would be more just and more filled with goodness and drenched in love.

But the gospel properly understood does lead to those things, and had we distinguished the "gospel" from the "Plan of Salvation," we wouldn't have gotten ourselves into all these motivational ploys. If we preach the Plan of Salvation as the gospel, we will find ourselves doing everything we can to get people motivated or, to use words from earlier, bucking up our efforts to get more people into column three, The Discipled. But, if we learn to distinguish gospel from Plan of Salvation, we will discover an altogether different world. I am convinced that because we think the gospel is the Plan of Salvation, and because we preach the Plan of Salvation as the gospel, we are not actually preaching the gospel. To make this more serious, what we are in most need of today, especially with a generation for whom the Plan of Salvation doesn't make instinctive sense, is more gospel preaching that sets the context for the Plan of Salvation. (More of that later too.)

While we are at this, a brief word about gospel, kingdom, and Plan of Salvation. Young pastors are at work today preaching, teaching, and embodying Jesus' vision for the kingdom of God, and nothing has been more revitalizing for many today than the kingdom vision of Jesus. What many are asking me is how to preach the "gospel" or how to "evangelize" people when it comes to the kingdom of God. "How do you," I've been asked hundreds of times, "evangelize people into the kingdom?" (I now suggest they read my book *One. Life: Jesus Calls, We Follow.*) But the problem I have with the question is that when people ask it, they use terms in unbiblical ways: when they use "evangelize" they mean "Plan of Salvation," and this gets us spinning in circles immediately. But kingdom and Plan of Salvation are like gospel and Plan of Salvation. They are two different sets of categories. The kingdom vision of Jesus isn't simply or even directly about the Plan of Salvation, though the kingdom vision entails or implies or involves the Plan of Salvation, and without the Plan of Salvation the kingdom doesn't work.

The struggle here is trying to wedge the Plan of Salvation into the kingdom vision, something Jesus doesn't do quite the way many would like him to have done. Why do we struggle here? Because we've equated "gospel" with "Plan of Salvation," and that means we are forced to equate "kingdom" with "Plan of Salvation." Worse yet, we are forced to decide. Many have opted for either kingdom or Plan of Salvation. But if we learn to distinguish these terms, we won't have to force "kingdom" into "Plan of Salvation" or "Plan of Salvation" into "kingdom" or choose between the two. (Again, more of this later too.)

THE METHOD OF PERSUASION

Now our fourth and final big category: *the Method of Persuasion* is how we have learned to "package" the Plan of Salvation in order most powerfully and successfully to persuade people to respond. I am referring here to two things: the specific biblical elements (like God's love and grace and faith) and the bundling of those elements into a rhetorical shape.

The preferred method of persuasion for many, if not most, begins with God's grace but quickly moves to the final judgment, hell, and the wrath of God. This second move uses terms that have a way of laying down a sense of ultimacy to our message and a way of grabbing the hearers' attention. But others think it more vital to show, embody, and proclaim the astounding love and grace of God and

> I remember seeing a particular diagram as a youth.
> It was a drawing that represented two sides and a
> deep gorge running down the middle. On one side
> was mankind trapped in sin, on the other was God
> in all his goodness. But there was no way to connect
> the two sides. Until the teacher would draw a cross
> bridging one side to the other, and illustrating how
> the death and resurrection of Jesus brought mankind
> into a right relationship with God.
>
> *"Esther"—a student*

pray that God's grace will warm the heart of those who listen. But this must be emphasized once again: our preferred Method of Persuasion and the gospel are not one and the same. I find many today who think the "gospel" we hear in our evangelistic tracts or in altar call sermons is the one and only gospel the church preached from the very beginning. We need perhaps to be reminded of the past.

A history of evangelistic preaching, which I have but sampled in my research for this book, shows that methods shift and conform to the needs of the evangelist and the audience. First, the sermons of Peter and Paul in Acts are not the same as the methods used in the history of the church, though we should be on guard to see that our gospel conforms to theirs.

Second, perhaps the earliest surviving example of gospeling after the apostles is now found in what is called *The Epistle of Diognetus.*[9] This letter has three prongs: to undercut idolatry, to distance the Christian faith from Judaism, and to present the gloriousness of Jesus Christ and the utter love and mercy of God for humans. There is much in common with the Gentile sermons of Paul in Acts 14 and 17, but this text unmistakably looks like a late second-century tractate on evangelism.

Third, the Reformation created new emphases, and nothing is perhaps more reformational in evangelistic focus than Thomas Cranmer's famous *A sermon on the salvation of mankind, by only Christ our Saviour, from sin and death everlasting.* There is one focus in this sermon, written to be read in all the churches of England in order to teach salvation, namely, to pull humans from trusting in themselves and to encourage them to learn to trust in Christ alone in order to find justification before God.[10] This is a very Reformation kind of gospel preaching.

Fourth, no matter where you dip into Wesley's sermons, you will end up with his clear teaching on the fullness of salvation and the necessity of faith in order to be justified and sanctified.[11]

Four eras we have seen, then — four different orientations to evangelism. Our method, then, is not the only method the church has ever used.

Note that we must distinguish the elements of the gospel from the bundling of those elements into a method of persuasion. But we cannot equate our Method of Persuasion — or Wesley's or Cranmer's for that matter — with the gospel itself. In fact, in light of what this study will conclude later, Figure 3 represents what has happened in our salvation culture. *The Plan of Salvation and the Method of Persuasion have been given so much weight they are crushing and have crushed the Story of Israel and the Story of Jesus. This has massive implications for the gospel itself.* I will say more about the Method of Persuasion in the rest of this book, but I want to raise a red flag right now: our Method of Persuasion is shaped by a salvation culture and is designed from first to last to get people to make a decision so they can come safely inside the boundary lines of The Decided. I will contend this method needs serious revision.

These four categories form two units. The Story of Jesus belongs to the Story of Israel/the Bible and only makes sense in that story. The Plan of Salvation and Method of Persuasion belong to each other. One of them is the theory and the other one the implication.

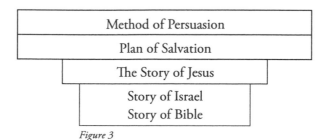

Figure 3

> The gospel I received was very simple,
>> it was very straightforward,
>> and there were no questions asked
>> because you need to do one simple thing, be a
> Christian....
>> I would simply call the gospel I received John
> 3:16, because that is the only verse from the New
> Testament that seemed to matter.
>
>> *"Rose"—a student*

The four need to be distinguished. But because we have crushed the Story of Israel and the Story of Jesus under the interpretation of the last two big ideas—the Plan of Salvation and the Method of Persuasion, and I confess I've done the same—the gospel has lost its edge and its meaning. Nothing proves this more than the near total ignorance of many Christians today of the Old Testament Story. One reason why so many Christians today don't know the Old Testament is because their "gospel" doesn't even need it! I hope that claim jars you into attention. The emailer who asked me the question "What's Messiah got to do with it?" reveals this very problem.

I will contend in the pages that follow that the word gospel *belongs to one and only one of our four sets of terms, and I will contend that it belongs to the Story of Jesus as the resolution of Israel's Story.* Once we get this straight and see the difference between "gospel" and "salvation," we will be able to develop a "salvation culture" that finds its only true home in a "gospel culture." But we've got some work to do to get there, and it begins with a set of questions many of us are asking:

What was the original gospel?

Or,

What was the apostolic gospel?

Or,

What was the gospel Jesus preached?

Or,

What was the gospel of the New Testament?

CHAPTER 4

THE APOSTOLIC GOSPEL OF PAUL

IT ALL DEPENDS on where you begin. A dad of a friend of a friend of my son (and it's actually a little more involved than that) is a golf course superintendent of a private country club. One day he told me to give him a call some Sunday evening and he'd let me play the course on a Monday—all alone—when the course was closed to members. So, I took him up on it and gave him a call. He told me what time to show up and where to park (so as not to create suspicion). Then he asked me a simple question: "Do you need me to tell you the course layout?" I was pumped about playing the course and not a little happy that I would play free. Since I had played so many courses in my life, I said, "No, Jim, I'll figure it out."

It was 6:30 a.m. when I got to the course, parked, grabbed my clubs, and walked up past the clubhouse to the first tee. Two problems complicated the situation. First, there were no tee markers that said "Hole #1." I immediately said to myself, "Of course not; this course is private, and the members know the course and don't need tee markers." The second problem was that there were no maps because there were no scorecards on the tee box. I thought again, "Of course not; members of this course get cards inside the clubhouse."

Then a third problem: there were three tee boxes near the club house and that meant to play the first hole first I had three choices. I made my choice, and for four holes I thought I was on the weirdest layout for a golf course I'd ever seen. As I got up on the fifth tee Jim drove up in his cart and said, "Wow, Scot, you must have gotten here early."

That question made it clear something was up because I hadn't gotten to the course any earlier than he suggested. So I asked Jim, "What do you mean?"

His response: "Scot, you're on #14." (I thought I was on #5.) He made a bone-crushing bit of humor: "I asked if you needed me to tell you the layout, and you said you didn't need it." With a big laugh he said, "You did! Get in the cart and I'll get you a card and we'll give you a new start." Then he said it all: "Golf courses don't make sense unless you begin at the right place."

He's right, and Jim's point is even more true when it comes to mapping our understanding of the gospel. Where to begin? The best place to begin is the *one place in the entire New Testament where someone actually comes close to defining the word* gospel. First Corinthians 15 is that place.

THE APOSTOLIC GOSPEL TRADITION

One of the biggest advantages of this one-of-a-kind definition of the gospel is that many scholars think it is also among the "oldest" set of lines in the entire New Testament. Scholars think this was the oral tradition about the gospel that every New Testament apostle received and then passed on. First Corinthians 15 is nothing less than a lifting up of the curtains in the earliest days of the church; it tells us what everyone believed and what everyone preached. This passage is the *apostolic gospel tradition.*[12] Thus...

Before there was a New Testament ...

Before the apostles were beginning to write letters ...

Before the Gospels were written ...

There was the gospel.

In the beginning was the gospel.

That gospel is now found in 1 Corinthians 15.

If we don't begin here, we will make a big mistake. To emphasize just how important this appeal to the apostolic gospel tradition by Paul, we should recall that Paul had had a one-of-a-kind experience of God's saving grace in his Damascus Road encounter with the exalted Lord, Jesus the Messiah. So overwhelming was this experience that Paul will later say *his gospel* was a personal revelation from God himself (Gal. 1:13–16). So clear was that revelation from God that he bluntly declares that he didn't need even need confirmation from the apostles themselves.

All of this emphasis by Paul is on his own uniqueness and the special revelation he had from God . . . but when it comes to defining the gospel, Paul is a square conservative. Instead of expressing the gospel in his own terms, he simply recites the tried and true gospel of the church's tradition. It's like asking the world's most famous theologian to state his or her theology in summary form and, instead of getting a personal statement, the theologian says, "I believe in God the Father, maker of heaven and earth, and in. . . ." That is, instead of giving you his or her own special framing of theology, the theologian gives you the Apostles' Creed. That's exactly what Paul did when he was asked to set out the "gospel": he quoted tradition.

1 CORINTHIANS 15 IN THREE PARTS

It will be useful for what follows to break Paul's words into three parts: A, B, and C. Part A is the introduction, and Part B defines the gospel. But because many think 15:20–28, after more than a dozen verses of interruption, continues Paul's "gospel statement," I'll include them too as Part C. The boldface will be clarified in what follows. It is too easy for those accustomed to the Bible to skip passages when quoted in books like this, so I'm asking you to read these verses carefully. This is where Paul began, and it is where we will begin. (We will show later why it is wise to begin here even when we ask if Jesus preached the gospel.)

A

Now, brothers and sisters, I want to remind you of the gospel I preached to you, which you received and on which you have taken your stand. By this gospel you are saved, if you hold firmly to the word I preached to you. Otherwise, you have believed in vain (15:1–2).

B

*For what I received I passed on to you as of first importance: that Christ died for our sins **according to the Scriptures**,*

that he was buried,
*that he was raised on the third day **according to the Scriptures**,*
and that he appeared to Cephas, and then to the Twelve. (15:3–5)

C

*But Christ has indeed been raised from the dead, the firstfruits of those who have fallen asleep. **For since death came through a man, the resurrection of the dead comes also through a man. For as in Adam all die, so in Christ all will be made alive.** But each in turn: Christ, the firstfruits; then, when he comes, those who belong to him. Then the end will come, when he hands over the kingdom to God the Father after he has destroyed all dominion, authority and power. For he must reign until he has put all his enemies under his feet. The last enemy to be destroyed is death. **For he "has put everything under his feet." Now when it says that "everything" has been put under him, it is clear that this does not include God himself, who put everything under Christ.** When he has done this, then the Son himself will be made subject to him who put everything under him, so that God may be all in all* (15:20–28).

This definition of "gospel" by the apostle Paul is the place to begin, and if we begin here, we will both find the meaning of "gospel" and we will have a map that will show how to navigate the rest of the New Testament and church history! If we begin here, we take the first step in creating a gospel culture. One could expound this text for pages and pages, but that is not needed here. Instead, I want to focus on just a few points.

EIGHT OBSERVATIONS ABOUT THE GOSPEL OF PAUL
"THE GOSPEL I GOSPELED"

In paragraph A (1 Cor. 15:1–2) *Paul connects himself to the Corinthians by means of the gospel.* The gospel, he says, is the "good news that *I* proclaimed." The Greek says it in a way that deserves notice: *to euangelion ho euēngelisamen*—or, "the gospel *I* gospeled." The gospel that Paul gospeled is more than that: it is also the gospel the *Corinthians* "received" and the gospel "on which [they] have taken [their] stand." Furthermore it is the gospel through which they are being "saved." The gospel of Paul saves and sustains. Yet one more time Paul emphasizes their gospel connection in the last complete line of paragraph A: "the word *I preached to you*" could be translated like this: "which word I gospeled to you." Our first observation is simple: it's all about "gospel."

THE TRADITIONAL GOSPEL

Paragraph B (1 Cor. 15:3–5) elaborates Paragraph A, and it does so through one word: the word "you received" (15:1). This word (*parelabete* in Greek) refers to the authorized tradition of the apostles that they had mastered (or had mastered them) and which Paul himself "received" (15:3, *parelabon*, same Greek verb). Paul then "passed on" that same gospel tradition to the Corinthians so they would have the authentic gospel. We need perhaps to pause to remind ourselves again what Paul is saying: he is saying that the gospel he gospeled is the authentic, reliable gospel of the apostles — he both received that gospel and passed it on. He's no innovator when it comes to the gospel.

And what is the authentic traditional gospel that Paul the apostle passed on to the Corinthians so they could receive it? Paragraph B tells us just that.

THE GOSPEL DEFINED

The authentic apostolic gospel, the gospel Paul received and passed on and the one the Corinthians received, concerns these events in the life of Jesus:

> that Christ died,
> that Christ was buried,
> that Christ was raised,
> and that Christ appeared.

The gospel is the story of the crucial events in the life of Jesus Christ. Instead of "four spiritual laws," which for many holds up our salvation culture, the earliest gospel concerned four "events" or "chapters" in the life of Jesus Christ.

We perhaps need to remind ourselves of something at the grassroots level: the word *gospel* was used in the world of Jews at the time of the apostles to *announce* something, to *declare* something as good news — the word *euangelion* always means good news. "To gospel" is to herald, to proclaim, and to declare something about something. To put this together: the gospel is to announce good news about key events in the life of Jesus Christ. To gospel for Paul was to tell, announce, declare, and shout aloud the Story of Jesus Christ as the saving news of God.

RESOLUTION OF ISRAEL'S STORY

Observe in paragraphs B and C above, especially the words that are in boldface type, *that the gospel Story of Jesus Christ resolves or brings to completion the Story of Israel as found in the Scriptures (our Old Testament)*. The important words used are "according to the Scriptures." The apostolic gospel is an "according-to-Scriptures telling of the Story of Jesus."

Anyone with a reference Bible can sit down with any of Paul's letters, and after reading a paragraph or two look up the cross references to see how often Paul's words are drawn from the deep wells of Israel's Scriptures. Paul explicitly cites the Old Testament more than one hundred times, and the number of implicit allusions and echoes in his letters boggles the mind.[13] In fact, Paul's imagination for understanding and preaching and teaching the gospel was shaped by the Story of Israel. Sometimes it's like a battering ram, as in Romans 3:10–18, where he cites five different passages in quick succession; other times it's a single passage, as in Galatians 3:6–9, where he is expounding texts from Genesis 12 and 15; at still other times it's subtle, as in 2 Corinthians 3:17–4:6, where Paul's play with words like Spirit, Lord, glory, and light evokes a number of passages, themes, and ideas from Israel's Scriptures. But you can't get away from it: Paul's gospel—better yet, the early Christian gospel—is rooted in the Scriptures.

The Story of Jesus Christ, then, isn't a story that came out of nowhere like the Book of Mormon, and it isn't a timeless set of ideas as with Plato's philosophical writings. The Story of Jesus Christ is locked into one people, one history, and one Scripture: it makes sense only as it follows and completes the Story of Israel. Darrell Bock, in his book *Recovering the Real Lost Gospel,* provides a scintillating example of how this Old Testament Story is at work in everything that can be called gospel.[14] I was struck how Bock begins his book: the gospel starts with a promise. What promise? Relationship in the Spirit. My heart pounded page after page as I read Bock's book because time and time again he gets it: the gospel is the resolution and fulfillment of Israel's Story and promises.

Once again, the "good news" of this gospel is that Israel's Story has now reached its resolution in Jesus Christ. This brings us back one more time to Figures 2 and 3 in chapter 3. Because the "gospel" is the Story of Jesus that fulfills, completes, and resolves Israel's Story, we dare not permit the gospel to collapse into the abstract, de-storified points in the Plan of Salvation.

SALVATION FLOWS FROM GOSPEL

This distinguishing of "gospel" from Plan of Salvation sometimes wrinkles the faces of my readers and listeners. So, let's make this clear: *salvation — the robust salvation of God — is the intended result of the gospel story about Jesus Christ that completes the Story of Israel in the Old Testament.* Paul uses a Plan-of-Salvation expression in his definition of gospel, and remember paragraph B is his own definition of gospel: "for our sins." Paul connects "for our sins" to "Christ died," showing one more central distinctive of the gospel: an emphasis on the cross as forgiving (and atoning).

We must say something vitally important to preserving a gospel culture: Paul does not articulate *how* Jesus' death did something "for our sins." He only tells us *that* Jesus actually died "for our sins." However we tell the Story of Jesus, that story must deal with "sins," and it must deal with those "sins" as something "for which" Jesus died. We can tell this story in a number of ways — and I'm thinking right now of Brenda Colijn's richly textured new book that explores images of salvation in the Bible[15] — but the story must aim at showing that the gospel *saves.*

My own preferred way to describe the comprehensiveness of the saving death of Jesus is to see that three things happened in that death:

Jesus died

(1) *with* us (identification),

(2) *instead of* us (representation and substitution), and

(3) *for* us (incorporation into the life of God).

That is, he first of all entered fully into the human condition — and not just our sinfulness but the fullness of our condition.

Second, he died our death as our representative and as a substitutionary death. That is, he stood in our place and shouldered the punishment due us for our sins, and that punishment according to the uniform witness of the Bible is *double death*, both a physical death and a spiritual/eternal death.

Third, his death did something *for our good*: his death procured forgiveness of sins, reconciliation with God, justification before God's tribunal—and I'll sidestep for now the comprehensiveness of this term, ransoming us from our slaveries and liberating us from all that entraps us. Ultimately, Jesus' death (and resurrection) leads us into the very presence and life of God. I believe this and more are at work when Paul says "for our sins." But the one thing is clear to me from this statement in 1 Corinthians 15: Paul is not locking salvation to one and only one image.

Paul says Jesus died for our sins "according to Scriptures," and it is my instinct, and perhaps yours, to dash back to the atoning passage of the Servant in Isaiah 53:10–12. But Paul does not chase to that text in 1 Corinthians 15 because he appears instead to be pointing us to the whole of the Old Testament's witness to atonement. Here, then, we'd have to begin with the sacrificial system and Moses, and Yom Kippur and even Passover. Only then can we get into texts like Isaiah 52 and 53, though we'd want to include such a passage as particularly clear.

Christian theologians have long debated "atonement theories," and I myself have weighed in.[16] We are not driven to any one of the theories by the expression "for our sins," but we are led to see that each of them in its own way has the power to unveil the saving impact of Jesus' death. It is better to expand our sense of what God has done "for our sins" than to lock onto one and only one theory. What Paul says was enough for the apostles—this is the apostolic gospel tradition—is enough for us today: Jesus died "for our sins."

I can't resist spelling this out a bit. A good example of seeing the saving effects and affects of the gospel is Galatians 4:4–6:

> But when the set time had fully come, God sent his Son, born of a woman, born under the law, to redeem those under the law, that we might receive adoption to sonship. Because you are his sons, God sent the Spirit of his Son into our hearts, the Spirit who calls out, *"Abba*, Father."

Another text is 1 Corinthians 6:11:

> And that is what some of you were. But you were washed, you were
> sanctified, you were justified in the name of the Lord Jesus Christ
> and by the Spirit of our God.

The terms used there describe the personal and corporate impact,
or affects, of the gospel itself: Jesus redeems and adopts and sends the
Spirit and sanctifies and justifies. These are the sorts of things the
apostles meant when they said Christ died "for our sins."

A Complete Story

Perhaps it struck you as you read Paragraphs A, B, and C above.
Perhaps it didn't. But what we need to put on the table as quickly as
possible in gospeling is that the gospel of the apostle Paul was about
the whole of Jesus' life, or what Brenda Colijn calls the "whole career
of Christ":[17] *the Story of Jesus Christ is a complete story and not just a
Good Friday story.*

No matter how central the cross is to the Story and to the Plan of
Salvation, we need to keep in mind that the story is more than the
story of the cross. Jesus didn't just die. The Story of Jesus includes,
by implication, the life of Jesus (birth, teachings, actions), but Paul's
focus is the last week and beyond. Paragraph B tells the Story of Jesus
in four lines:

> the death of Jesus,
> the burial of Jesus,
> the resurrection of Jesus,
> and the appearances of Jesus.

Furthermore, the Story of Jesus continued beyond the appearances,
and many (I'm one of them) judge it likely that the "gospel" Paul
received and Paul preached and the Corinthians received did not
end with paragraph B (at 15:5), but continued to the end of all ends
in paragraph C (vv. 20–28). In other words, there are reasons to
think the gospel of Paul included the ascension of Jesus, the second
coming of Christ, and the full consummation of the kingdom when
God becomes all in all.

It is common today to emphasize the death of Jesus as recon-
ciling, forgiving, atoning, propitiating, redeeming, ransoming, and

> I would go to a camp every summer that would have what they called "Cross Night." They would show a very graphic video of the death of Christ and when emotions were high would tell everyone that if they wanted to accept Christ there were people around the room that would help them do so. The video stopped after Jesus died and the resurrection wasn't even spoken of.... I was taught that I was saved because of Christ's death; the resurrection was almost a bonus, and the second coming was something everyone should be scared of.
>
> *"Denise"—a student*

justifying; not much gospeling deals with the burial, the resurrection, the appearances, or the final consummation. Our use of "Pastor Eric" above is a good example, because Pastor Eric thinks nothing outside the death (and resurrection) matters for the gospel itself. Because we are prone to ignore anything other than the death, with perhaps a glance at the resurrection, let me give a word about each of the other elements.

The *burial* of Jesus sets up the resurrection, but one has to hear such things as Acts 2:29, where Peter says David was buried and reminds his listeners that David's tomb is right there in Jerusalem. In the burial Christ entered fully into our death, and in that burial the church has taught that Christ visited/ransomed the prisoners in hell (cf. 1 Peter 3:18–22).[18]

The *resurrection* evokes a theology of justification (Rom. 4:25) and even more of God's eschatological irruption into space and time—the new creation (2 Cor. 5:17) and the arrival of the final general resurrection.[19] The appearances evoke a real bodily resurrection (see John 21) and a profound apologetic for that belief, and the exaltation, second coming, and final consummation reveal a theology of Jesus as Lord and Judge and God as having a Plan for History that arrives at its destiny after this long journey, when all things are in their proper place as God rules. What this means is that the gospel is a whole-life-of-Jesus story, not just a reduction of the life to Good Friday. In my judgment, soterians have a Good-Friday-only gospel.

THE JESUS OF THE GOSPEL

There is a Person at the very core of the gospel of Paul, and until that Person is put into the center of centers in Paul's gospel, we will not comprehend his—scratch that—the apostles' gospel accurately. The gospel Story of Jesus Christ *is a story about Jesus as Messiah, Jesus as Lord, Jesus as Savior, and Jesus as Son.* It is sometimes forgotten that "Christ" is the Greek translation of the Hebrew word *Messiah.* The word *Messiah* means "anointed King" and "Lord" and "Ruler." Lord means, well, "Lord," and the word *Son* here certainly means the anointed king of Israel, as in Psalm 2. So, the emphasis here in the gospel is that Jesus is Lord over all.

But he is king as a result of battle. The Story of Jesus, according to paragraph C, involves Jesus' triumphal victory over "all dominion, authority and power." This victory goes even deeper and broader: Jesus, Messiah and Lord and Son, will conquer "death" as well. Any reading of 1 Corinthians 15, then, will immediately fasten our ideas on Jesus as the center of the Story.

One of my favorite expressions of the centrality of Jesus in the gospel can be found in 2 Corinthians 1:18–22, where Paul tells us

Implicitly, in the theology I often heard, Jesus did not really need to be raised since the mission of Jesus was to forgive us of our sins and that was accomplished on the cross.

The resurrection only theologically counted for style points.

As for the general resurrection of the dead, I almost never heard anything about that . . .

in many ways the gospel I was taught does not end in the same place Paul's gospel ends.

"Jay"—a student

that God's inscripturated and storied promises became a loud trumpet-like "Yes!" in Jesus, and we are to confess him by saying "Amen!"

> But as surely as God is faithful, our message to you is not "Yes" and "No." For the Son of God, Jesus Christ, who was preached among you by us — by me and Silas and Timothy — was not "Yes" and "No," but in him it has always been "Yes." For no matter how many promises God has made, they are "Yes" in Christ. And so through him the "Amen" is spoken by us to the glory of God. Now it is God who makes both us and you stand firm in Christ. He anointed us, set his seal of ownership on us, and put his Spirit in our hearts as a deposit, guaranteeing what is to come.

If I had to sum up the Jesus of the gospel, I would say "King Jesus." Or I would say "Jesus is Lord" or "Jesus is Messiah and Lord." As King, as Messiah, and as Lord, Jesus is the Savior, or Liberator, "from our sins."

END OF ALL ENDS

Finally, debates swirl about 1 Corinthians 15:28, the last sentence in our paragraph C: "When he has done this, then the Son himself will be made subject to him who put everything under him, so that God may be all in all."

One thing is clear and certain: *the story will end with God the Father being God for all and in all and through all, and his Son will be glorified as the One through whom God is glorified.* At that point we reach glory and the end of the Story. The long story from creation to consummation, from the garden to the city of God, from earth as temple to the Lamb as temple, the story that marches from Adam to Abraham to Moses to David to Jesus and then the spread of the story, the gospel story about Jesus, will reach its goal when God is for everyone whom God should be for everyone.

One could say the end of ends in 1 Corinthians 15:28 completes the task God gave to humans in the opening chapter of the Bible on day six (creation of humans). Humans were given just one charge: to govern this world as God's representatives. So, in 1 Corinthians 15:28, when we are finally connected to God in this eternal union with God through his Son, humans will be doing exactly what God intended for his creation. God will be God and we will be God's people—and the whole Story will be about God.

PASTOR TOM

Pastor Tom has a completely different idea of what the gospel is than did Pastor Eric. And Pastor Tom is one of the few who have examined afresh what the New Testament actually says about the gospel. Pastor Tom, usually called Tom Wright or N. T. Wright, in an important book called *What Saint Paul Really Said*, discusses the meaning of the word *gospel* in Paul's writings. His opening salvo aims directly to the point we have been making about a salvation culture dwarfing a gospel culture:[20]

> Many Christians today, when reading the New Testament, never question what the word [gospel] means, but assume that, since they know from their own context what they mean by "the gospel," Paul and others must have meant exactly the same thing.

Tom then observes that the term has come to mean *ordo salutis*, roughly what we explained as the Plan of Salvation,[21] and is supposed to be ...

- a description of how people get saved;
- of the theological mechanism whereby,
- in some people's language, Christ takes our sin and we his righteousness [double imputation];
- in other people's language, Jesus becomes my personal saviour;
- in other languages again, I admit my sin, believe that he died for me, and commit my life to him.

And Tom goes on:

> ... if you hear a sermon in which the claims of Jesus Christ [as Lord] are related to the political or ecological questions of the day, some people will say that, well, perhaps the subject was interesting, but "the gospel" wasn't preached.

Tom's next set of observations put into eloquent prose what we have just discovered in what Paul means by gospel in 1 Corinthians 15:

> I am perfectly comfortable with what people normally *mean* when they say "the gospel." I just don't think it is what Paul means. In other words, I am not denying that the usual meanings are things that people ought to say, to preach about, to believe. I simply wouldn't use the word "gospel" to denote those things.

Exactly. Wright is pointing a scolding finger at the identification of the gospel with the Plan of Salvation. But Wright, who is more in touch with the actual texts of the New Testament than many, knows that the word *gospel* does not mean this. What then does "gospel" mean for Wright?

To answer this question, Tom enters into descriptions of two backgrounds to Paul's usage of the term *gospel*, including both that powerful set of images from Isaiah as well as the characteristic empire gospel of Rome. For Paul, the word *gospel* is connected to the Story of Israel/Bible in his Roman context. Most importantly, the word *gospel* in the first century context was an *announcement*: "to announce that YHWH was king was to announce that Caesar is not."

But Tom goes farther and in so doing appears to be the foil of Pastor Eric, and he clearly states that "gospel" is not the Plan of Salvation: the gospel "is not, then, a system of how people get saved. The announcement of the gospel results in people getting saved.... But 'the gospel' itself, strictly speaking, is the narrative proclamation of King Jesus." "Or, to put it yet more compactly: Jesus, the crucified and risen Messiah, is Lord." A few pages later Wright unpacks this meaning in a more general and universally applicable sense: "The 'gospel' is for Paul, at its very heart, *an announcement about the true God as opposed to the false gods.*"

The question we need to ask is this: Which Pastor—Eric or Tom—gets this right? Which one of these is closer to what the New Testament actually says? One more pastor first.

PASTOR GREG

We began this chapter by asking where we are to begin, and we contended that the singularly most important place to begin is 1 Corinthians 15. I stand by that, and in the following chapter the wisdom of that choice will become clear. But it is obvious that others begin elsewhere. Pastor Greg Gilbert, a pastor-teacher at Capitol Hill Baptist Church in Washington, D.C., has a new and exceptionally clear book called *What Is the Gospel?* Gilbert believes the place to begin is the book of Romans, in particular Romans 1–4.[22] In effect, Gilbert's gospel is what I learned as a child as the Romans Road to Salvation, and Pastor Greg and Pastor Eric are more or less on the same page when it comes to the meaning of the gospel.

Gilbert's gospel is the Plan of Salvation, and so he finds four points to latch onto in Romans 1–4: first, humans are accountable to God, which emerges from his reading of Romans 1 especially. Second, the problem humans have is that we have rebelled against God, and here he fastens onto Romans 1:23; 2:1; 3:9, 19; and of course 3:23. Third, the solution to humanity's rebellion problem is the sacrificial death and resurrection of Jesus, and no finer passage in the entire Bible witnesses to this than Romans 3:21–26. And, fourth, humans can be included in this salvation by faith alone, and again we find this in that most central of Pauline passages, in Romans 3:22. Full agreement. Four points: God. Man. Christ. Response. But the question is this: Is this the Plan of Salvation or is this the apostolic gospel?

There is not time here to engage in a lengthy discussion of all the items I have checked in the margins as I read Gilbert's book on two separate occasions, but I will make these points. First, Gilbert is not alone, but he is an exceptionally clear example of equating the gospel with the Plan of Salvation. I believe the equation is a mistake.

Second, my criticisms include these: Gilbert has minimized the structural significance of 1 Corinthians 15; he has focused only on the salvation bits in the evangelistic sermons in the book of Acts; he has not given sufficient emphasis to the Story of Israel as yearning for resolution in Jesus as the Messiah and Lord as the framing story for how to understand gospel; and this Story of Israel is the driving focus of the book of Acts' sermons and 1 Corinthians 15.

Furthermore, I believe the fundamental issue Paul is dealing with in Romans is not simply the personal salvation issue but the problem of how God joins together Jewish believers and Gentile believers into the one church of Jesus Christ. Also, Gilbert has overcooked the holiness of God and nearly eclipsed the gracious love of our Father (read his second chapter to see this overemphasis).

In addition, Gilbert would have done well to give Romans 1:1 – 5 more attention. This is how Paul opens the book of Romans, and these opening verses show that Paul's understanding of gospel fits what is said in 1 Corinthians 15: it is a declaration of the Story of Jesus as King and Lord. Notice the emphasis on the Story of Israel coming to completion as the framing story for what the gospel is:

> Paul, a servant of Christ Jesus, called to be an apostle and set apart for the gospel of God — *the gospel he promised beforehand through his prophets in the Holy Scriptures regarding his Son,*[23]
>
> [Now notice the theme of Jesus as the Davidic Messiah:]
> who as to his earthly life was a descendant of *David,*
>
> [Observe how quickly Paul connects resurrection to gospel and that Jesus is Lord:]
> and who through the Spirit of holiness was *appointed the Son of God in power by his resurrection from the dead: Jesus Christ our Lord.*
>
> [And this lordship theme is extended by Paul, as we see constantly in the sermons in Acts, to emphasize that the gospel is for Jews and Gentiles so they can become one holy church:]
> Through him we received grace and apostleship to call all the *Gentiles* to the obedience that comes from faith for his name's sake. And you also are among those *Gentiles* who are called to belong to Jesus Christ.

Please recognize that I'm not saying Gilbert's expositions of specific points are wrong even if I would frame things differently. What I am saying is that Gilbert begins in the wrong place because he equates gospel with salvation — the Plan of Salvation — and does not therefore see the fundamental gospel to be a declaration about Jesus Christ as the resolution of Israel's Story. He has processed the story through the lens of the Plan of Salvation, but the gospel of 1 Corinthians 15 processes the gospel through the lens of Israel's Story, finding its resting place in Jesus Christ. In doing this Gilbert has omitted fundamental layers of the gospel.

Furthermore, I want to emphasize that I see as much gospel in Romans as does Gilbert. I see the entire book to be a "gospeling" or a "gospelizing" of the Story of Israel as it makes its impact on how to understand (1) the relationship of Jews and Gentiles since Jesus has been exalted to the right hand of God, and (2) the nature of that salvation that flows out of the gospel proclamation that Jesus is Messiah and Lord for both Jews and Gentiles. In the eloquent words of Tom Wright that I quoted earlier:

> I am perfectly comfortable with what people [like Gilbert] normally *mean* when they say "the gospel." I just don't think it is what Paul means. In other words, I am not denying that the usual meanings are things that people ought to say, to preach about, to believe. I simply wouldn't use the word "gospel" to denote those things.

Summary

We must now sum up this chapter: the gospel for the apostle Paul is the salvation-unleashing Story of Jesus, Messiah-Lord-Son, that brings to completion the Story of Israel as found in the Scriptures of the Old Testament. To "gospel" is to declare this story, and it is a story that saves people from their sins. That story is the only framing story if we want to be apostolic in how we present the gospel. We can frame the "gospel" with other stories or categories, but there is one holy and apostolic story, and it is the Story of Israel. That is the apostolic framing story for the gospel.

This story begins at creation and finally only completes itself in the consummation when God is all in all. This is Paul's gospel, and while it includes and encompasses the Plan of Salvation and leaves open how one might construct a Method of Persuasion, the gospel of Paul cannot be limited to or equated with the Plan of Salvation. The four lines of Paul's gospel are about the Story of Jesus. Every time Paul mentions "gospel" in his letters (and he does so some seventy-five times), he is referring to this four-line gospel. And many times Paul uses "shorthand" by simply saying "gospel" or "my gospel" or the "gospel of salvation" or even "Christ crucified." But he always means this gospel—the gospel of the full, saving Story of Jesus resolving the Story of Israel, the one we found in shorthand in 1 Corinthians 15 and which then is fully expounded in the Gospels themselves (more on that later).[24]

This leads to a warning, and it is one that animates much of this book: the Plan of Salvation can be preached apart from the story, and it has been done for five hundred years and two thousand years. When the plan gets separated from the story, the plan almost always becomes abstract, propositional, logical, rational, and philosophical and, most importantly, de-storified and unbiblical. When we separate the Plan of Salvation from the story, we cut ourselves off the story that identifies us and tells our past and tells our future. We separate ourselves from Jesus and turn the Christian faith into a System of Salvation.

There's more. We are tempted to turn the story of what God is doing in this world through Israel and Jesus Christ into a story about *me and my own personal salvation.* In other words, the plan has a way of cutting the story from a story about God and God's Messiah and God's people into a story about God and one person — me — and in this the story shifts from Christ and community to individualism. We need the latter without cutting off the former.

Cutting the plan from the story leads to a salvation culture that is entirely shaped by "who is saved and who is not saved." That culture is important, and I believe in salvation in Christ. But, that culture is designed by God to be a subculture and not the dominant culture. The dominant culture is the gospel culture. And a gospel culture is one shaped by the Story of Israel and the Story of Jesus Christ, a story that moves from creation to consummation, a story that tells the whole Story of Jesus and not just a Good Friday story, and a story that tells not just of personal salvation but of God being "all in all." It tells the story that Jesus, not any human ruler, is the Lord over all.

You must now be asking this simple question: How did the gospel get taken over by this Plan of Salvation? To answer this question we have to move forward from the New Testament and skip through centuries of church history. Since this question is asked of me so often, we have to pause now to consider that very question before we go back to the New Testament.

CHAPTER 5

How Did Salvation Take Over the Gospel?

I DID NOT GROW UP in a creedal world. My church was so nervous about creeds and reciting creeds and prayers that we never even recited the Lord's Prayer together. Zeus would have tossed thunderbolts at us had we even tried to recite the Apostles' Creed. We were nervous about any creed other than "I believe in the Bible." So I had to break through the boundaries of my own conscience when I began to learn about the creeds. I succumbed to the creeds only after considerable study and thought and prayer and resistance. But I now see the creeds, especially the Apostles' Creed and the Nicene Creed, or the Niceno-Constantinopolitan Creed, as fundamental to the faith of all Christians.

But there is something far more important to learn about the creeds than that they are part of our heritage. Careful attention to words has now convinced me that "creed" and "gospel" are intimately connected, so intimately one can say the creed is the gospel. Perhaps you are shocked that I could even connect "creed" to "gospel." This will become clearer by the end of the chapter.

Though I've been aware of the words used in the creed for a long time, it was in reading a book by Ted Campbell called *The Gospel in Christian Traditions* that a historical reality about the creeds and the gospel dug its way into my bones and brought new life to my own personal faith.[25] After I read Ted Campbell's book, I read (or slogged my way through) Jaroslav Pelikan's *Credo*.[26] Both Campbell and Pelikan discuss how the earliest Christians arranged what they believed into what is now called the "Rule of Faith" (in Latin, *regula fidei*). And this Rule of Faith developed over time to become the three principal creeds of the Christian faith: the Apostles' Creed, the Nicene Creed, and the Chalcedon Definition. In studying this history I landed on something that I think is uniformly ignored by most Christians—that the earliest Christians were developing a "gospel" culture. Put in summary form here is the big picture we will sketch in this chapter:

> First Corinthians 15 led to the development of the Rule of Faith, and
> the Rule of Faith led to the Apostles' Creed and Nicene Creed.
> Thus, 1 Corinthians led to the Nicene Creed.
> Thus, the Nicene Creed is preeminently a gospel statement!

But this gospel framing of the creed was revised later—and that revision led from a gospel culture to a salvation culture.

In studying this history and development, I began to see this simple observation: *the classic universal (or "catholic") creeds of the church flesh out Paul's articulation of the gospel in 1 Corinthians 15:3–5*, or paragraph B above. Here are Paul's words again:

> For what I received I passed on to you as of first importance: that Christ died for our sins according to the Scriptures, that he was buried, that he was raised on the third day according to the Scriptures, and that he appeared to Cephas, and then to the twelve.

Let me say this with emphasis: the creeds articulate what is both implicit and explicit in Paul's grand statement of the gospel in 1 Corinthians 15. This point must be emphasized because it may not even be known to many Christians today: *1 Corinthians 15 is the genesis of the great Christian creeds*. This means these creeds were designed from beginning to end not to banter back and forth about speculative doctrines *but were shaped to clarify the gospel itself.* One can say with accuracy that the Nicene Creed is an *exegesis* or *exposition* of the gospel tradition of Paul in 1 Corinthians 15. That's a simple observation that deserves a hundred qualifications once one enters into the intensity of the debates in the first four centuries, and once one entertains the complexity of the issues involved. There wasn't simply a straight line from 1 Corinthians 15 to Nicea, but that line is still apparent in that history.

I have always encountered people who boldly announce to me that they are "noncreedal" and even say "I don't believe in the creeds" because of their next words: "I believe in the Bible." I respond with one question, and I think I ask this question because I too was at one time one of their number: "What line or lines in the Nicene Creed do you *not* believe?" I've never had one say they didn't believe any of it, though some have had enough substance in their anti-creedalism to wonder if "one holy catholic and apostolic church" just might mean "Rome," and since they're not Catholics, they wonder if they believe that line. Other than that, though, there's nothing there *not to believe*. In fact, denial of the creeds is tantamount to denying the gospel itself because what the creeds seek to do is bring out *what is already in the Bible's gospel*. I will show why I say that below.

The Story from Paul to Nicea

Let's begin with one of the earliest theologians and martyrs, Ignatius. On his trip—one might call it a "march of triumph"—across Turkey (Asia Minor) toward Rome to be put to death,[27] Ignatius wrote seven letters to churches in Asia Minor. In the letter *To the Trallians* 9.1–2, he expresses what he believes about Jesus Christ:

> who is of the stock of David who is of Mary,
> who was truly born, ate and drank,
> was truly persecuted under Pontius Pilate,
> was truly crucified and died in the sight of the beings of heaven, of earth and the underworld,
> who was also truly raised from the dead.

While Ignatius is not explicitly quoting from 1 Corinthians 15, his words bear a striking similarity to how Paul summed up the Story of Jesus. These words could not have been said this way without Paul having said what he did and without the apostles forming that "gospel tradition" that they passed along. Yes, there are words and ideas here that are not found in Paul, and yes, Ignatius is interacting with both Judaizing and docetic tendencies, which lead him to express the gospel in terms of the suffering (*pathos*) and resurrection of Jesus.[28] But one can say Ignatius makes explicit what he thought was implicit in the apostolic gospel.

In about AD 190, Irenaeus framed the earliest and clearest *regula fidei*, and his words too show a striking resemblance to the words of the apostle Paul, and I have highlighted those Pauline echoes in italics:[29]

> this faith: in one God, the Father Almighty, who made the heaven and the earth and the seas and all the things that are in them; and in one Christ Jesus, the Son of God, who was made flesh for our salvation; and in the Holy Spirit, who made known through the prophets the plan of salvation, *and the coming, and the birth from a virgin, and the passion, and the resurrection from the dead, and the bodily ascension into heaven of the beloved Christ Jesus, our Lord, and his future appearing from heaven in the glory of the Father to sum up all things and to raise anew all flesh of the whole human race.*

As with Paul, Jesus' entire life is at work: the incarnation "for our salvation," the birth, the passion, the resurrection, the bodily ascension, and his future appearing. And like Paul, Irenaeus sees a story with a goal: "to sum up all things and to raise anew all flesh of the whole human race." Irenaeus's *regula fidei*, or creed, is shaped by Paul's gospel. Creed and gospel are connected.

A decade or so later another early theologian, Tertullian, provided yet another creedal statement that derives from Paul's gospel statement. Here are Tertullian's words and, though he's getting some of his stuff from the gospel of John, I italicize the words that show connection to the apostle Paul's gospel statement in 1 Corinthians 15:[30]

> We, however, as we indeed always have done and more especially since we have been better instructed by the Paraclete, who leads men indeed into all truth, believe that there is one only God, but under the following dispensation, or *oikonomia*, as it is called, that this one only God has also a Son, His Word, who proceeded

from Himself, by whom all things were made, and without whom nothing was made.

Him we believe to have been sent by the Father into the Virgin, and to have been born of her—being both Man and God, the Son of Man and the Son of God, and to have been called by the name of Jesus Christ; *we believe Him to have suffered, died, and been buried, according to the Scriptures, and, after He had been raised again by the Father and taken back to heaven, to be sitting at the right hand of the Father, and that He will come to judge the quick and the dead;* who sent also from heaven from the Father, according to His own promise, the Holy Ghost, the Paraclete, the sanctifier of the faith of those who believe in the Father, and in the Son, and in the Holy Ghost.

That this rule of faith has come down to us from the beginning of the gospel, even before any of the older heretics, much more before Praxeas, a pretender of yesterday, will be apparent both from the lateness of date which marks all heresies, and also from the absolutely novel character of our new-fangled Praxeas.

One notable observation remains: in the third paragraph, Tertullian claims that this "rule of faith" (again, *regula fidei*) came down to him—that he "received" it as did the Corinthians and Paul—"from the beginning of the gospel." That is an overt connection to Paul's own statement and to the apostolic gospel tradition. Creed and gospel are connected.

One more before we get to the Nicene Creed, and this one comes from Hippolytus about one or two decades after Tertullian.[31] A candidate for baptism, stripped naked, in the order of children, men, and then women, was asked a series of questions, and then the baptisand, or person being baptized, was to make a confession. Roughly, this is the sacred act of being questioned before baptism was permitted:

[Do you believe in God the Father Almighty?]
Do you believe in Christ Jesus, the Son of God, who was born of the Holy Spirit and the Virgin Mary, and was crucified under Pontius Pilate, and was dead and buried, and rose again the third day, alive from the dead, and ascended into heaven, and sat down at the right hand of the Father, and will come to judge the living and the dead?

Do you believe in the Holy Spirit, in the holy church, and in the resurrection of the body?[32]

Again, observe that the confession required for baptism was a confession rooted in the gospel statement of Paul in 1 Corinthians 15, showing once again that creed and gospel are united.

Perhaps what is most notable is that the gospel statement of Paul was almost entirely about Jesus Christ, while the growing church tradition about creeds became increasingly Trinitarian as it filled in the lines of what was assumed (or believed to be assumed) by the original apostolic gospel.[33] What is most notable, though, is this: the so-called second article of the creed, the lines about Jesus, *are always shaped by what Paul said about the gospel in 1 Corinthians 15:1–5, 20–28.* First Corinthians 15 was not just a casual statement by Paul; it was the apostolic definition of the gospel that Paul himself passed alongside the other apostles.

Finally, we come to the Nicene Creed (AD 325),[34] and it doesn't take but a moment's notice to see that the Son clauses are rooted in 1 Corinthians 15.

We believe in one Lord, Jesus Christ,
    the only Son of God,
    eternally begotten of the Father,
    God from God, Light from Light,
    true God from true God,
    begotten, not made,
    of one Being with the Father.
    Through him all things were made.
    For us and for our salvation
    he came down from heaven:
    by the power of the Holy Spirit
    he became incarnate from the Virgin Mary,
    and was made man.
    For our sake he was crucified under Pontius Pilate;
    he suffered death and was buried.
    On the third day he rose again
    in accordance with the Scriptures;
    he ascended into heaven
    and is seated at the right hand of the Father.

He will come again in glory to judge the living and the dead,
and his kingdom will have no end.

The same connection to 1 Corinthians 15 is seen in the second article in the Apostles' Creed:[35]

And [I believe] in Jesus Christ his only Son our Lord; who was conceived by the Holy Ghost, born of the Virgin Mary, suffered under Pontius Pilate, *was crucified, dead, and buried; he descended into hell; the third day he rose again from the dead; he ascended into heaven, and sitteth on the right hand of God the Father Almighty; from thence he shall come to judge the quick and the dead.*

Much more could be said about this sketch of creedal history but this one thing needs to be observed: *the Nicene Creed, as well as the* regula fidei *leading up to it, and the creeds that flowed out of Nicea, are not to be seen as exercises in theological sophistry or speculation but profoundly gospeling events.* To recite the creed for these early Christians was not to dabble in the theologically arcane but to articulate and confess—aloud and often—the gospel itself. To deny these creeds was to deny the gospel.

We have traveled a considerable distance from Paul's letter to the Corinthians in the heart of the first century to Nicea in the fourth century, but we had to traverse this landscape to make two points clear: the gospel is the Story of Jesus as the completion of the Story of Israel as found in the Scriptures, and that gospel story formed and framed the culture of the earliest Christians. That culture was first and foremost shaped by this gospel, and within that gospel culture the subculture of a salvation culture was formed. Those who were saved were those who embraced the gospel Story of Jesus Christ.

But I don't want to suggest that the early churches were perfect nor that the first four centuries were ideal. There never was an ideal church because the ideal is the kingdom, and that is yet to come. In fact, those early churches had their own sorts of problems, including theological debates that somehow managed—against all claims to gospel love and peace and justice—to inflict punishment and even capital punishment on dissenters. Their disputes escalated into such levels of acrimony that their confessed unity of the church became a wish instead of a reality. They set in motion a sacramental process that far too often made salvation automatic for the baptized. They capitulated to Constantine so much that the church and the Roman empire became an invisible wall of indifference. "Crusades" is all one has to say, even if there are careful nuances now being put on what happened (and what did not).

No, I don't want to suggest the gospel culture created a beautiful gospel church or an overwhelming number of genuine disciples of Jesus. All I want to contend for is that the first four centuries were shaped by a gospel culture that derived directly and profoundly from the apostolic gospel tradition. But something happened that has led to the contemporary superficial perception of gospel and reduction of salvation to personal decision and has all but wiped out the gospel culture of Jesus and the apostles.

How, then, did we get from this gospel culture to our salvation culture?

WHAT HAPPENED?

You may now be asking, as I have myself numerous times, *What happened?* How did we develop a salvation culture out of a gospel culture? How did "evangelicals" become "soterians"? Or, when did the "gospel" become the Plan of Salvation? It began in many ways with Augustine, but its more focused beginning was in the Reformation, though it did not happen during the Reformation. We can pinpoint the documents themselves that both provide evidence for the shift that was underway and that also provide the foundation for creating a salvation culture. Those two documents, one from the Lutheran wing and one from the Calvinist/Reformed wing, are the *Augsburg Confession* and the *Genevan Confession*.

But before we get there, my own confession. Cutting out the inevitable nonsense that accompanies everything humans do, including Calvin's wretched decisions that led to the burning of Servetus, Luther's wretched beliefs about Jews and his wretched decisions about the Anabaptists, and wretched tendencies of the Anabaptist sectarian to think of themselves as the only people of God, I believe the Reformation was a profound work of God that both enlivened the church and altered Western European history for the better. The singular contribution of the Reformation, in all three directions—Lutheran, Reformed, and Anabaptist—was that the gravity of the gospel was shifted toward human response and personal responsibility and the development of the gospel as speaking into that responsibility.

This is not to deny the important and real differences between these three movements, but it is to say that the one thing that emerged in each was a heavy sense of the need for personal salvation. I do not mean that such was not found in Roman Catholicism; rather, the Reformation said, in effect, that the "gospel" must lead to personal salvation—and the rest is history.

But with that emphasis, regardless of how important it was and remains, came a price. The gospel culture began to shift to a salvation culture. Our contemporary equation of the word *gospel* with the Plan of Salvation came about because of developments from and after the Reformation. When I read today's thin and superficial reductions of the gospel to simple points, I know that that could never have happened apart from the Reformation. I also know that it didn't happen during the Reformation itself but as a result of the Reformation's reframing of the apostolic gospel-become-creed.

Now, briefly, the two documents mentioned above. I begin with the Augsburg Confession. The Reformation statements focused on the elements of the Christian faith that led to their differences with the Catholic Church, but in so doing the Reformation churches did not deny the Nicene Creed. Instead, they reframed the faith in ways that provided a lens through which they now saw the creed itself.

In 1530, Philip Melanchthon presented to Charles V at the Diet of Augsburg a confession built on conclusions that were forming among the Lutheran Protestants. I draw attention here to the order and substance of this confession, which need to be seen over against the classical order and substance of the Nicene Creed. Nicea framed things through God the Father, God the Son, and God the Holy Spirit, and the God the Son articles were derived from 1 Corinthians 15. The Augsburg Confession converted the order of the "articles" into sections on *salvation and justification by faith*. It is precisely here that a "gospel culture" was reshaped into a "salvation culture" or,

better yet, "justification culture." Here are the central categories of
the Lutheran confession:

God as Triune [as at Nicea]
Original sin [major reshaping idea]
The Son of God [as with Nicea and Chalcedon, with a clear
    understanding of a satisfaction and propitiation of God's
    wrath]
Justification by faith

Then the Augsburg Confession covers the office of ministry, the
new obedience, the church, baptism, the Holy Supper, confession,
repentance, sacraments, order in the church, church usages, civil
government, the return of Christ to judge, freedom of the will, the
cause of sin, and a lengthy discussion of faith and good works, and
it concludes with the cult of the saints before it discusses matters
about which the Reformers were in serious dispute. I wish to make
only one point: this Lutheran confession framed the gospel in terms
of salvation. It would not be inaccurate to say that the gospel "story
became soteriology," or the Story of Israel/Bible/Jesus became the
System of Salvation.

The Reformation did not deny the gospel story and it did not
deny the creeds. Instead, it put everything into a new order and
into a new place. Time and developments have somehow eroded the
much more balanced combination of gospel culture and salvation
culture in the Reformation to where today a salvation culture has
eclipsed the gospel culture.

The Genevan Confession of 1536, set out by William Farel and
John Calvin, like the Augsburg Confession, had both predecessors
and subsequent clarifications, such as the Second Helvetic Confession (1566) or the Westminster Confession (1646), but those aren't
our concern here. What is important is that the genius of the Reformation's focusing of the gospel on salvation by faith alone comes to
the fore also in the Genevan Confession. Like the Augsburg Confession, the Genevan Confession is framed even more by a "salvation
culture." Hence, here are the central articles that express the heart of
the Reformed perspective on the gospel:

The Word of God
The one and only God
The law of God alike for all
The natural man — total depravity
Man by himself is lost
Salvation in Jesus
Righteousness in Jesus
Regeneration in Jesus
Remission of sins necessary for the faithful

Once again, the list continues with other items of the faith: all our good in the grace of God, faith, invocation of God only and intercession of Christ, prayer intelligible, the sacraments of baptism and the Holy Supper, human traditions, the church, excommunication, ministers of the Word, and magistrates.

Even more so with Calvin (and William Farel) than with Luther, the gospel story is set into a new framing story, the story of salvation. Contemporary evangelicalism, especially in the United Kingdom and the United States, has absorbed this Reformation (salvation) story. To put it lightly, in many cases it has not only absorbed but done plenty of subtraction and reframing. There are huge pockets of evangelicalism where this profound Reformation reframing is little more than four simple (and thin) points: God loves you, you are messed up, Jesus died for you, accept him and (no matter what you do) you can go to heaven. My contention is not that the Reformation created that sort of gospel, but that the Reformation's reshaping of the gospel story has made it a pale shadow of what it ought to be.

In fact, no one can read either Luther or Calvin and not observe that they operated with both a profound gospel culture and a profound salvation culture. I have no desire to blame them or the Reformation for the soterians or a "salvation culture." I thank God for the Reformation. But I do want to point out that the seeds for the contemporary and mostly evangelical four-points approach to the gospel could not have happened were it not for the Reformation's shifting from the story to soteriology.

Evangelicalism's Experiential Focus

So let's push a bit into what happened after the Reformation and examine the evangelical movement.[36] To be a true-blue evangelical in our heritage or to be accepted into the membership of a church in the evangelical tradition, one has to give witness to one's personal experience of salvation. The Puritans sometimes called this personal statement of faith a "relation"; but whatever one may want to call it, the experience of personal salvation is the threshold-crossing event, and the ability to give witness to that event is required for full acceptance. John Wesley expresses in pristine words the evangelical experience:[37]

> In the evening I went very unwillingly to a society in Aldersgate Street, where one was reading Luther's Preface to the Epistle to the Romans. About a quarter before nine, while he was describing the change which God works in the heart through faith in Christ, *I felt my heart strangely warmed.* I felt I did trust in Christ, Christ alone for salvation, and an assurance was given me that he had taken away *my* sins, even *mine*, and saved *me* from the law of sin and death.

To this day in most evangelical churches, both where they baptize infants and where adult baptism is practiced, a potential member is asked to meet with deacons or elders or the pastor to witness to one's experience of salvation. Though it need not sound like Wesley's or other archetypal conversion stories, the story will be examined to see that it is real and personal. While contemporary descendants of these groups may not have the rigor or create the anxiety that some of the early Puritan Congregationalist churches created, the person who listens to the testimony of faith in today's churches is expected to be able to discern if the signs of grace or conversion are present. This culture of personal salvation and personal testimony captures what I mean by a salvation culture. For this culture, it is the ability to witness personally to the experience of conversion that matters most. Once one has had this experience, it's all over . . . until the final party arrives.

Pastor Dallas

Like Pastor Tom Wright, Dallas Willard does double duty: he's both a professor and a pastor. Willard discusses this reduction of gospel to salvation and the reduction of salvation to personal forgiveness and gives it a potent and damning label: *the gospel of sin management*.[38] Willard uses the image of a bar code for this salvation culture: if we get the right barcode—say the right thing, make the right confession, have the right experience, make the right decision, etc.—when God scans the barcode, the lights will go off and we will be safe. Willard proposes salvation culture's problem in this way:

> If you ask anyone from that 74 percent of Americans who say they have made a commitment to Jesus Christ what the Christian gospel is, you will probably be told that Jesus died to pay for our sins, and that if we will only believe he did this, we will go to heaven when we die.

And he continues:

> In this way what is only one theory of the "atonement" is made out to be the whole of the essential message of Jesus [the gospel].

> What does it mean in this setup to "believe"?

> But for some time now the belief required to be saved has increasingly been regarded as a totally private act, "just between you and the Lord." Only the "scanner" would know.

The difference between what Calvin and Luther (as well as Wesley) taught and what Willard excoriates in his book is so dramatic one has to wonder if some today are reading the same Bible.

From the enhancement of a gospel culture with a profound emphasis on salvation we have now arrived at the ability for a person to be able to say he or she has had the right experience. And that experience far too often is nothing more than "I'm a sinner; Jesus, take my place." A gospel culture will have none of it, nor will a proper sense of salvation. I leave the last words here for Willard:

> What must be emphasized in all of this is the difference between trusting Christ, the real person Jesus, with all that that naturally involves, versus trusting some arrangement for sin-remission set up through him—trusting only his role as guilt remover.

These are the words of his that haunt the pages of this book, and here he is pointing at the "you" of evangelicalism:

> Your system is perfectly designed to yield the result you are getting.

And here it comes with full force:[39]

> "Gospels of Sin Management" presume a Christ with no seri-
> ous work other than redeeming humankind ... [and] they foster
> "vampire Christians," who only want a little blood for their sins but
> nothing more to do with Jesus until heaven.

Dallas Willard takes us then into the kingdom vision of Jesus, but
his concern, like mine, is about a salvation culture that has eclipsed
a gospel (and discipleship) culture.

This is perhaps all, if not more than, we need for our point,
which is that the "gospel culture" that ruled the church from the
time of Jesus to the Reformation and which was shaped and built
on 1 Corinthians 15, was reshaped during the Reformation—for
mighty good reasons I might add—into a salvation culture. One
more time, let me emphasize this: I'm not idealizing the early church
or the medieval church. I have plenty of beefs with developments
during those periods, including struggles over the increasing cen-
teredness of Marian themes, the momentous shifts in centralizing
power that led, tragically, to such things as indulgences, as well as
a near automatic sacramentalization that impeded the message of
personal response to the gospel. I don't want to call into question
the God-led significance of the Reformation. So, I do not dispute
the need for clarifying salvation and making its personal application clear and necessary. Rather, what happened is the apostolic gospel culture was reframed in such a way and so successfully, largely
as a result of the powerful evangelistic culture of evangelicalism in
American revivalism and then later in America's culture war between
fundamentalists and modernists, that today we are losing contact
with the gospel culture.

We need to regain contact with the gospel culture in a way that
we do not lose the salvation culture, but to do that we have to begin
at the beginning one more time. We began this book by asking
whether Jesus preached the gospel. Now that we have examined both
the apostolic gospel and how that gospel shifted to a system of salvation, we can ask this question about Jesus with fresh eyes.

If we believe that Paul's statements in 1 Corinthians 15 are the
gospel, then we have to ask a slightly different question than many

think they are asking when they ask if Jesus preached the gospel. More often than not, folks are asking if Jesus preached the Plan of Salvation instead of asking if he preached the "gospel." They are asking, in effect, if he came to establish a "salvation culture" or a "gospel culture." In our next two chapters we want to look at the four Gospels and at Jesus, and we will suggest that, in fact, Jesus did preach the gospel — but this all hinges on what we mean by the word *gospel*.

CHAPTER 6

THE GOSPEL IN
THE GOSPELS?

WE BEGAN THIS JOURNEY with Paul. I admit that it may sound backward to go first to Paul and only then to Jesus and the Gospels. I wanted to begin this study with a sketch of Jesus' view of the kingdom of God, but I knew that what I would emphasize would sound strained until we encountered how centrally Jesus is in the gospel of 1 Corinthians 15. But now, in light of what Paul says about the gospel in 1 Corinthians 15, we have been given a whole new angle on this term. Until we can clear from our minds the idea that the gospel and the Plan of Salvation are the same thing, we cannot find the principle of unity in the entire history of the church. But, once we do show the relation of gospel and salvation, which we sketched in what we said about 1 Corinthians 15, we suddenly discover that not only did Paul preach a gospel different than many of us think, but we find that Paul's gospel was the same as Jesus' and — in fact — the same as everyone's in the first century.

So our contention is that examining 1 Corinthians 15 all over again leads us now to ask an entirely different question. It would be good for us to remind ourselves how the questions have been asked in the past. Everyone observes that there's a shift from Jesus to Paul. Jesus focused on kingdom but Paul focused, at least in Romans and Galatians, on justification. So, the former questions were these: Did Paul preach kingdom? Or, did Jesus preach justification? With a little bit of twisting or turning — in fact, sometimes with a lot of twisting and turning—we could get Jesus to preach justification or Paul to preach kingdom. I suggest this gets it wrong because in each case it defines "gospel" as either kingdom or justification. My contention is that the gospel is bigger than both terms.

The gospel, I am arguing, is declaring the Story of Israel as resolved in the Story of Jesus. That was Paul's gospel, and it was the apostolic gospel tradition, and that gospel shaped everything in the church until the Reformation, at which time that gospel was slightly shifted and eventually—and it took the better part of two or three centuries for this to happen—gospel was submerged under salvation so much that gospel was equated with Plan of Salvation. But now that we have seen what Paul actually preached, which again was the declaration that the story has been completed in Jesus himself, we are led to a whole new question. Rather than ask if Paul preached kingdom or if Jesus preached justification, we now ask this question:

Did Jesus claim Israel's Story was fulfilled in himself?

Or, even more directly,

Did Jesus preach himself?

And, if he did,

Then Jesus too preached the gospel!

We can frame this in a number of ways, so here's one more: *Did Jesus make his kingdom message center on his own role in the Story of Israel?* If we answer "Yes" to any of these questions, we are saying that Jesus preached the gospel.

Once we learn to frame the question in this manner, everything falls into place, and this leads me to the question we have not yet asked or answered. It's an important question, and more important than perhaps many realize. Here goes: *Have you ever wondered why the first four books of the New Testament are called "the Gospel"?*

THE GOSPELS AND THE GOSPEL

I will not forget the day I was sitting at my desk pondering the first four books of the New Testament as a whole in preparation for a class lecture, when I naïvely asked myself a question that only a first-year college student would ask (and then only because he or she is naïve). I answered the question in a way that ushered me for a moment into glory because it was one of those experiences where mind and body and soul all clicked. Here was my question:

Why did the early Christians call these books "the Gospel"?

I knew they didn't focus on anything like what we call the Plan of Salvation, and they surely aren't shaped by our Method of Persuasion. No, all they are—and all four of them are like this—is story after story about Jesus and the power of God at work in and through him. So, as I sat there pondering that question of why they called Matthew, Mark, Luke, and John "the Gospel," the answer came rather quietly in stages:

Maybe they are the gospel.

Well, yes, they are the gospel.

Yes, the Gospels are the gospel!

What clicked was that I suddenly realized that Paul's "gospel" was the Story of Jesus completing Israel's Story, and the reason the early Christians called Matthew, Mark, Luke, and John "The Gospel according to" Matthew and Mark and Luke and John was because they knew each of those Gospels told that very same Story. Paul *and* the Gospels tell the Story of Israel coming to completion in the Story of Jesus. The apostolic gospel, the tradition the apostles passed along, can be found in the Gospel of Matthew and Mark and Luke and John. It may seem patently obvious, but it's not to most: they called these books "the Gospels" because they are the gospel.

If you want to read the gospel,

hear the gospel,

or preach the gospel,

read, listen to, and preach the Gospels.

PASTOR JOHN

And now to a fourth pastor. Pastor John Dickson is an evangelist, a pastor, and a professor in Australia, and I am grateful his books and videos are impacting his native country. His newest book, *The Best Kept Secret of Christian Mission: Promoting the Gospel with More Than Our Lips,*[40] is one of the finest books on evangelism and the gospel I have read. I want to avoid any more introduction and hunker down on how he understands the word *gospel*:

The core content of the gospel therefore goes something like this:

- Jesus' royal birth secured his claim to the eternal throne promised to King David.
- Jesus' miracles pointed to the presence of God's kingdom in the person of the Messiah.
- Jesus' teaching sounded the invitation of the kingdom and laid down its demands.
- Jesus' sacrificial death atoned for the sins of those who would otherwise be condemned at the consummation of the kingdom.
- Jesus' resurrection establishes him as the Son whom God has appointed Judge of the world and Lord of the coming kingdom.

This statement is close to Tom Wright's and, like Wright's view, a long way from Pastor Eric and Pastor Greg. For Pastor John gospeling "involves recounting the deeds of the Messiah Jesus." It is a declaration of the "kingdom of God, the establishment of his rightful kingship over the world, which will one day be fully disclosed in a new creation." And resonating through his chapter is a response to whether or not Jesus preached the gospel: "The [Four] Gospels and the gospel are one." It is that last statement that will now take us into the theme of this chapter: *The Four Gospels and the gospel are one.*

THE GOSPEL, NOT THE GOSPELS

Perhaps we need to remind ourselves of a basic fact. The early Christians weren't describing the first four books as a kind of literature, as if "gospel" was a *genre* of literature and already had a number in the Dewey Decimal System of ancient libraries. No, we need to say this loud and clear: they didn't call the first four books of the New Testament the "Gospels." Instead, they called each one of them the "Gospel." They were saying there was one Gospel, but it was written down in four versions, the (one) Gospel according to Matthew, Mark, Luke, and John. In fact, to call them "Gospels" as we now do so casually is to suggest that there was more than one gospel.

F. F. Bruce, the dean of evangelical New Testament scholars for much of the twentieth century once observed that to call the first four books of the New Testament the "four Gospels" was "an impossible expression in New Testament times."[41] While each of those books would have been called "the Gospel," no one referred to them in the plural (e.g., "we read in the four Gospels") for more than a century after they were written. St. Augustine once corrected himself on this very point: "In the four Gospels," he said, "or better in the four books of the one Gospel."[42] Why make this point? Because authors of these books did not see themselves as authors or biographers of Jesus so much as *witnesses to the one gospel* when they told the Story of Jesus.

The single biggest, and really one-and-only-one, idea dominating, if I may now according to our custom use the plural, the Gospels, is this: *the Gospels are about Jesus, they tell the Story of Jesus, and everything in them is about Jesus.* This is so obvious we sometimes forget it. The evangelists (notice what we call them!), then, were telling the Story of Jesus as the gospel because it was the gospel. As Paul saw the Story of Israel completed in the Story of Jesus, so the four Gospels, showing they are truly the gospel itself, focus as well on Jesus. Front and back, left and center, and middle—each of these Gospels is about Jesus.

To "gospel" is to tell the Story of Jesus. Pastor John says this so well: "All of the Scriptures point to the gospel, *but only the Gospels recount the gospel in all its fullness. The Gospels and the gospel are one.*"[43] His words are confirmed from the opposite end of the church spectrum, from Pope Benedict XVI: "To call the four accounts of Matthew, Mark, Luke and John 'Gospels' is precisely to express that Jesus himself, the entirety of his acting, teaching, living, rising and remaining with us is the 'gospel.' " And hear too the Pope's follow-up words: "Since Easter, the method of evangelization has been to tell men what we now read in the Gospels."[44]

What becomes patently obvious to the reader of any of the Gospels is that they do not tell us the Plan of Salvation, and neither do they offer to us a Method of Persuasion. Instead, they fit perfectly into what that great apostle Paul indicated because *they narrate the Story of Jesus in a way that shows that Jesus completes Israel's Story in a way that the story is a saving story.* Furthermore, they are lopsidedly oriented—in a peculiar manner for the ancient world—on the narrative of Jesus' last week. That is, they focus on the death and resurrection of the hero — Jesus — more than any story in ancient history. This also perfectly conforms to Paul's own emphasis: he doesn't say anything directly in 1 Corinthians 15 about the birth or life or teachings of Jesus, but he goes right for the death, the burial, and the resurrection.

But we dare not lose contact with the saving impact of the Story of Jesus as found in the Gospels. Martin Hengel, who was Germany's leading New Testament scholar for three decades, put it like this: "The story told in [the gospel of Mark] calls hearers to belief in the person who is described in it, Jesus, the Messiah and Son of God, and thus to eternal life; in other words it seeks to be wholly and completely a message of salvation."[45] Scotland's leading New Testament scholar, I. Howard Marshall, complements Hengel by speaking of the third gospel in the same terms: "Luke's purpose is not merely to narrate the deeds and words of Jesus but to show how these did in fact lead to the experience of salvation and to the formation of the community of the saved."[46]

But to see if the Gospels are the apostolic gospel, we need to do some fact checking. Do the four Gospels tell that same story of Jesus?

DEATH, BURIAL, AND RESURRECTION

It has been said over and over that Mark's gospel is a Passion story with an extended introduction. That is, Mark's gospel is almost 50 percent focused on Jesus' last week (Mark 10 – 16), and we could say that Mark has nine opening chapters that set us up for that last week. Most scholars today think Mark's gospel was the earliest one written and became, as it were, a template for Matthew and Luke — and even for John. Observe that the template they inherited was a template lopsidedly oriented toward the last week of Jesus. Why? Because that is the way to tell the gospel itself.

Mark's focus on the death and burial and resurrection is very gospel-like according to Paul's and the apostles' definition. A Greek reader feels this focus on the last week more than an English reader. The Greek reader encounters in Mark's gospel the Greek word *euthys*, usually translated "immediately," thirty-four times in the first nine chapters. I remember the first time I sat down to read Mark in Greek in one setting and realized, after a few chapters, that my heart was racing. I began to wonder why this was happening, so I paused to become more self-reflective. I soon realized it was because I felt Mark was in such a hurry to move from one event to the next, and this was experienced with the Greek word *euthys*. It is obvious to a careful reader of the second evangelist that *Mark couldn't wait to get Jesus to the cross!* Once Mark gets Jesus to the passion, the word *euthys* all but disappears. This word itself is a gospel-directed and gospel-directing word in Mark's gospel. Here are a few examples (I have italicized the English words that translate the Greek word *euthys*):

- Mark 1:10: *Just as* Jesus was coming up out of the water, he saw heaven being torn open and the Spirit descending on him like a dove.
- 1:12: *At once* the Spirit sent him out into the wilderness.
- 1:18: *At once* they left their nets and followed him.
- 1:20: *Without delay* he called them, and they left their father Zebedee in the boat with the hired men and followed him.
- 1:21: They went to Capernaum, and *when* the Sabbath came, Jesus went into the synagogue and began to teach.
- 1:23: *Just then* a man in their synagogue who was possessed by an impure spirit cried out.
- 1:28: News about him spread *quickly* over the whole region of Galilee.
- 1:29 – 30: *As soon* as they left the synagogue, they went with James and John to the home of Simon and Andrew. Simon's mother-in-law was in bed with a fever, and they *immediately* told Jesus about her.
- 1:42 – 43: *Immediately* the leprosy left him and he was cleansed. Jesus sent him away *at once* with a strong warning.

It's like Mark uses this word *euthys* as a herding instinct to keep his readers moving toward the last week of Jesus.

This perfectly illustrates why Mark opens up this book with these words: "The beginning of the *good news [or 'gospel'] of Jesus Christ, the Son of God*" (1:1). In this opening line Mark titles his book "the gospel" because he is "gospeling" in this book. What does that mean? That Mark is narrating the saving, forgiving Story of Jesus as the completion of Israel's Story. This, by the way, is why his very next words tell us that Israel's Story is coming to its resolution in John and Jesus:

> As it is written in Isaiah the prophet:
> "I will send my messenger [John] ahead of you,
>   who will prepare your way" —
> "a voice of one calling in the wilderness,
> 'Prepare the way for the Lord [Jesus],
>   make straight paths for him.'" (Mark 1:2 – 3)

Let's make this point clear: the gospel is the Story of Jesus as the completing Story of Israel. The first four books of the New Testament, the Gospels, are called "The Gospel according to ..." because they are telling that same story. And they each have the same emphasis on the death, burial, and resurrection of Jesus (see Matt. 19 – 28, Luke 18 – 24). John's gospel, though it has a different kind of structure, at least approximates what we find in the first three Gospels (the Synoptic Gospels), because at least from chapter 11 through 21 we have more or less a concentration on the last week. These three Gospels also have a heavy emphasis in the last-week narratives on the burial and especially the resurrection and appearances of Jesus.[47] This point must be emphasized because we are so stuck on the word *gospel* meaning Plan of Salvation. The Gospels are called "The Gospel according to ..." because they declare the Story of Jesus according to the apostolic script: the death, burial, and resurrection of Jesus — and this all according to the Scriptures.

ACCORDING TO THE SCRIPTURES

Another apostolic gospel theme is "according to the Scriptures." Paul said Jesus died and was raised "according to the Scriptures." Any real gospeling has to lay out the story of Scripture if it wants to put back the "good" into the good news.

No one does this any better than our first evangelist. Matthew's gospel famously begins with, of all things, a genealogy that ties Jesus to Abraham and to David, with a cryptic but clever use of "fourteen" generations (Matt. 1:1 – 17). The number fourteen comes from a Jewish method called *gematria*, which is to find significance in numbers. The name *David* is made up of three Hebrew consonants: *d-v-d*. Hebrew didn't have numbers as we do, but instead used letters both for letters and numbers. So if you add up d + v + d, or 4 + 6 + 4, you get 14. So, when Matthew organizes Israel's history into three groups of fourteen, he is showing that all of Israel's Story has a Davidic shape, and that Davidic Story comes to completion in the complete Davidic King, Jesus, son of Mary and Joseph, Messiah of Israel. There is so much of this "Old Testament fulfillment in the Gospels" it would not be difficult to write ten books on how the Old Testament, or Israel's Story, shaped each of the four Gospels.[48] One thinks of Matthew 1–2, which contains a series of events in Jesus' life that "complete" or "fulfill" Israel's prophetic Scriptures.

Now to Luke and the "according to the Scriptures" theme. One thinks of Luke's brilliant birth narratives in chapters 1 and 2, punctuated as they are by the beautiful songs often sung at Christmas: *Magnificat* and *Benedictus* and *Nunc Dimittis* (the songs of Mary, Zechariah, and Simeon). What needs to be noted here is that these three songs and these two chapters are loaded up with allusions and quotations from the Old Testament. In fact, they read as if someone had spent years soaking in the Scriptures and all of a sudden burst out with a set of poetic songs that bring the whole of Israel's Story to a completion in what God was doing in Mary and Zechariah and Elizabeth and Simeon and Anna—and especially in the two baby boys, John and Jesus. Be sure to sit down someday with a reference Bible and chase down all the Old Testament quotations and allusions in Luke 1–2. It can be a profound gospeling experience.

Our fourth evangelist, John, is an Old Testament kind of guy too, but John's gospel carries forward Israel's Story to Jesus in a way that takes fulfillment to a new level. At a breathtaking level, John shows how the principal institutions and feasts of Israel, those annual celebrations that told Israel's Story and that shaped both memory and identity for every observant Jew, find their own completion in Jesus. Thus, we have Jesus as the temple in John 2, the Sabbath in John 5, the Passover in John 6, the Feast of Tabernacles in John 7–10, and the Dedication in John 10:22–39.[49] As New Testament scholar R. N. Longenecker puts this theme together, in John's gospel we find the "representation of Jesus as the fulfillment of that which was symbolized by the feast[s]."[50]

This is but a sketch, but it's enough to ring the bell: the Gospels are gospel because they see the Story of Israel completing itself in the Story of Jesus. I would encourage readers of the Gospels to read a passage or a chapter and then to pause and ponder long enough to permit their knowledge of Israel's Story — the Old Testament Scriptures — to help them find connections between what the evangelists are saying and what the Old Testament told us. It's everywhere, and without this story-to-story way of reading the Gospels, one simply doesn't grasp what the evangelists were doing. With it the first four books become what they are called on the shelves of the church's library: the gospel.

FOR OUR SINS

One of the central elements of the gospel, according to the apostle Paul's statement in 1 Corinthians 15:3, is that "Christ died *for our sins.*" The Gospels, if they want to qualify as the gospel, must also speak about "for our sins." In fact they do, but they do so under so many terms and categories that it is hard to draw them all into the net. The word *sin* occurs forty-one times in the Gospels, and it is not accidental that in the opening chapter of the opening gospel we have an opening statement about who Jesus is. Matthew 1:21 says it this way: "She [Mary] will give birth to a son, and you [Joseph] are to give him the name Jesus, because he will *save his people from their sins.*" "Jesus" translates the Hebrew *Yeshua,* which means "YHWH is salvation." By naming Mary's son "Jesus," Joseph named him "Savior." From what was he saving people? "From their sins."

The profundity of this cannot be missed: "YHWH is salvation" has just become "God-in-flesh-salvation" and "Jesus-is-salvation." Israel — having failed to live up to a covenant calling and wrecked by disobedience, now mired in subjugation to Rome, blanketed with petty wars and ripping at the seams with religious and political infighting — would be rescued and the kingdom would come, and this would all occur through Mary's son. He would rescue Israel by saving Israel from the burden of its sins. John the Baptist, who himself preached repentance for the forgiveness of sins (Mark 1:4–5), announces in John's gospel words that echo the words of Matthew 1: "The next day John saw Jesus coming toward him and said, 'Look, the Lamb of God, who takes away the sin of the world!'" (John 1:29).

Both Judaism and the Gospels drew lines of accountability between one's sins and sicknesses, and so also forgiveness draws its own lines toward healing because the former created the latter. One thinks of what Jesus said to the paralyzed man in Matthew 9:2: "Take heart, son; your sins are forgiven." This breathtaking comment drew affirmative applause and negative astonishment, so Jesus heals the man and proves his case: he is, as Matthew 1 told us, the one who would rescue Israel from the penalties of sin, one of which penalties was sickness.

A third theme in the Gospels about "for our sins" can be found in the Last Supper narrative. Matthew's gospel deserves to be called gospel for this text alone: As Jesus passes the cup, he says, "This is my blood of the covenant, which is poured out for many *for the forgiveness of sins*" (Matt. 26:28). Matthew said Jesus would be called "Jesus" because he would save Israel from its sins; John the Baptist saw Jesus as the Lamb of God who removes the sins of the world; and Matthew's gospel tells us that in the final night with his disciples, Jesus *forgives by virtue of his self-offering on the cross*. His disciples partake in that forgiveness by believingly partaking in the cup (and eating the bread).

The apostolic gospel, the gospel that Paul "received" and "passed on" to the Corinthians, like every other apostolic church then and forever, is a gospel that has at its center that Jesus died "for our sins," and this death achieved the forgiveness of sins. As such, this story saves and brings people into the kingdom of God and ushers them into eternal life. John tells us that he wrote his gospel for this specific reason: "But these are written so that you may come to believe that Jesus is the Messiah, the Son of God, and that by believing you may have life in his name" (John 20:31). The "life" of which Jesus speaks here is the life that displaces the condition of sin.

But there's an incompleteness to this "for our sins" that John's "life" fills in. The apostolic faith is that Christ died for our sins, to be sure, but that death became effective over sins *because of the resurrection of Jesus himself from the among the dead.* Our sins bring death, and while Jesus' death enters into our death, that death is reversed into life by the resurrection. In that resurrection Jesus' death became effective to unleash the new creation. The cross gospel requires a resurrection gospel.

As Paul says it, apart from the resurrection we are "still in [our] sins" (1 Cor. 15:17). Paul's apostolic "for our sins" is tied to the death of Christ in that apostolic summary, but let us not forget — as we are so prone to do with our emphasis on the cross of Christ — that apart from resurrection the cross remains nothing more than an instrument of torture and suffering. This, too, is powerfully presented in the Gospels, not least in Matthew 27:51 – 53. When Jesus was crucified, indeed, at the moment of his death, Matthew records concerning this event:

> At that moment the curtain of the temple was torn in two from top to bottom. The earth shook, the rocks split and the tombs broke open. The bodies of many holy people who had died were raised to life. They came out of the tombs after Jesus' resurrection and went into the holy city and appeared to many people.

Death and resurrection are bound together to unleash an entire new world order, the new creation.

THE GOSPELS AS THE GOSPEL

The apostolic gospel, embedded in 1 Corinthians 15, announces the Story of Jesus as the completion of Israel's Story in the Scriptures in such a way that Jesus saves people from their sins. This is the apostolic gospel. The earliest Christians called the first four books of the New Testament "the Gospel according to ..." because they declare that very Story.

- The Gospels are all about Jesus.
- They are all about Jesus being the completion of Israel's Story.

- They are all about Jesus' death, burial, resurrection, exaltation, and future coming.
- They reveal that this Jesus, this Jesus in this very story, saves his people from their sin.

It is true and therefore doubly important for us to realize that these Gospels do not arrange the story into our own way of framing the Plan of Salvation, and neither do they format the story into our favorite Method of Persuasion. Instead, they declare the Story of Jesus, and that story is the saving, redeeming, liberating story.

We may have to speculate to come to this conclusion, but this sort of speculation is entirely reasonable. We have good reasons to think that the Gospels were written to embody the "gospeling" or the Gospel preaching of the apostles.[51] One could say the four Gospels are extensive commentaries on 1 Corinthians 15 or the apostolic gospel tradition. There is an early Christian tradition that informs us that the gospel of Mark puts into print (though not in an orderly or organized fashion) the preaching of Peter in Rome. Here's how the first church historian, Eusebius,[52] recorded that tradition:

> And the Elder used to say this:
> Mark became Peter's interpreter and wrote accurately all that he remembered the Lord had said or done, though he did not write these things down in order. For Mark himself neither heard nor followed the Lord but later on ... followed Peter. And Peter taught the Lord's sayings in an episodic form but not in an orderly fashion ... and so Mark did nothing wrong when he wrote out single points as he remembered them.

Whether that tradition is precisely accurate or not, it is at least true at the theological level: the four Gospels embody what the apostles remembered and taught about Jesus. We could even think about the connection of the apostolic gospel tradition in 1 Corinthians 15 and the Gospels as going in two different directions at the same time. On the one hand, the gospel preaching of the apostles could be reduced to 1 Corinthians 15:3–5, and, at the same time, we could say that 1 Corinthians 15:3–5 was expanded and expounded into the first four Gospels. Why can we say this? Because the gospel and the Gospels are one and the same.

Perhaps one odd verse—at least odd according to the way many of us understand the word *gospel*—will make this same point one more time. In Jesus' last week as told in the gospel according to Mark, we hear of a woman who anointed Jesus with a jar of costly ointment, which she poured extravagantly and gratefully on Jesus' head. Some heartless scrooges suggested that such extravagance could have been better spent on the poor, to which Jesus offered praise of the woman for prophetically anointing his body for his burial before he had even died. Then he says this: "Truly I tell you, wherever the gospel is preached throughout the world, what she has done will also be told, in memory of her" (Mark 14:9).

Why? Because Jesus assumes the preaching of the gospel will mean telling stories about the life of Jesus, *including this very story of the woman who had just poured oil on him.* I have had Christian students tell me that they know the gospel well but have never heard this story, and whatever you think of their reading habits, what this "never-heard-of-it" says is that gospel and the four Gospels are not connected tightly enough. We do know that in the earliest churches the leaders publicly read from the gospel weekly (see appendix 2), something we need to revive once again in our churches. It was this constant immersion in the Gospel[s] that created the potential for a gospel culture.

We have now reached a critical juncture. It is clear enough how Paul defined the gospel and it is clear enough why the first four books of the New Testament are called "the Gospels." But this sets the stage for the one question that many Christians today are asking, and the answer to this question matters intensively to many of us:

Did Jesus preach that gospel?

CHAPTER 7

JESUS AND THE GOSPEL

IT BEARS REPETITION because it is so hard for us to grasp. So many of us equate gospel with the Plan of Salvation that we have to train our minds to think through this over and over. The question we are asking is this: Did Jesus preach the gospel? But that does not mean, Did Jesus preach personal salvation or preach justification by faith (no matter how true and important those concepts are)? Instead, we have to move to a different plane. If the gospel is the saving Story of Jesus that completes the Story of Israel, the question is actually more refined: *Did Jesus preach that he was the completion of Israel's Story?*

If he did, Jesus preached the apostolic gospel, whether he preached the Plan of Salvation or not. So the gospel question is not, "Did Jesus preach the Plan of Salvation or justification by faith or personal salvation?" but, "*Did Jesus preach himself as the completion of Israel's Story in such a way that he was the saving story himself?*" This question will shape this chapter, and it will be like a one-note song that just goes on and on. We want to emphasize by repetition the centrality that Jesus gave to himself in his ministry and preaching.

This new question shifts the entire focus from the *benefits of salvation that we experience* to the *Person who himself is the good news*. Not long ago John Piper wrote a book with a rather quirky title that I think gets to the heart of what we are arguing in this book. His book was called *God Is the Gospel*. Here's what he meant: "The highest, best, final, decisive good of the gospel, without which no other gifts would be good, is the glory of God in the face of Christ revealed for our everlasting enjoyment."[53] What Piper calls "the glory of God in the face of Christ" is what I mean by "the Story of Jesus." The closer you get to the center of the Gospel, the clearer becomes the very face of Jesus. So, if I may retitle his book for this study, *Jesus Is the Gospel*. In spite of some important differences between what I'm arguing here and Piper's gospel book, we agree on this: the gospel is to declare something about a Person, about God in his revelation in Jesus Christ and about what God has done for us in Jesus Christ.

The question that 1 Corinthians 15 generates for us is this question: Did Jesus preach a gospel that concerned that same Person? To answer that we first explore Jesus' favorite term: kingdom.

KINGDOM

We begin with "kingdom" because Jesus overtly connects his mission, his vision, and his preaching with kingdom. Before we get to Jesus, though, we have to set the immediate stage. Three preliminary passages reveal that those closest to Jesus thought Israel's Story was coming to the big moment: Mary's *Magnificat* in Luke 1:46–55, Zechariah's *Benedictus* in 1:67–79, and John the Baptist's preaching of messianic repentance in 3:1–18. Each of these passages emerges breathtakingly from the messianic and kingdom expectations of Israel's Story, each of these concentrates on the completion of those themes in the births of John and Jesus, and each of these announces a completely new state of affairs for Israel. In particular, they announce a community marked by justice, holiness, peace, and love—but this community is clearly the community that sits at the feet of *Jesus*.

Each of these passages is all about Jesus in one way or another. Mary's song, the *Magnificat*, sees the entire sweep of God's covenant with Israel coming to completion in her baby boy, whom she will call Jesus and whom she hears is the Son of God and the King of Israel who will sit on David's throne. Zechariah's prophecy focuses on his prophet-son, but within his own words there is the prediction that the "horn of salvation" will rise in the "house of David," who will rescue Israel "from the hand of our enemies" and give us an endless reign of holiness and righteousness. That person is Jesus.

John, too, nearly three decades later, continues with the identical theme: he is the "voice" who speaks up for the one "who is more powerful than I," and that person will "baptize you with the Holy Spirit and fire." Kingdom for Mary, Zechariah, and John is a community ruled by a King, the Messiah. Kingdom isn't just a state of affairs, like justice and peace and love and holiness. Kingdom is a community made up of four features that shape the entire Story of Israel: God, king, citizens, and land. The king is Jesus, the citizens are those who follow Jesus, and the land is the place where they will embody the kingdom of God.

We are so accustomed to these passages we can easily miss the astounding claims being made: that Israel's Story has now found the amazing liberty of its final chapter. If you'd like to know what Jews thought the kingdom would be like, read Psalm 72, and I quote the whole of it because it brings into words the hopes of Israel for a king and his kingdom.

> Endow the king with your justice, O God,
>   the royal son with your righteousness.
> May he judge your people in righteousness,
>   your afflicted ones with justice.
> May the mountains bring prosperity to the people,
>   the hills the fruit of righteousness.
> May he defend the afflicted among the people
>   and save the children of the needy;
>   may he crush the oppressor.
> May he endure as long as the sun,
>   as long as the moon, through all generations.
> May he be like rain falling on a mown field,
>   like showers watering the earth.
> In his days may the righteous flourish
>   and prosperity abound till the moon is no more.
>
> May he rule from sea to sea
>   and from the River to the ends of the earth.

May the desert tribes bow before him
    and his enemies lick the dust.
May the kings of Tarshish and of distant shores
    bring tribute to him.
May the kings of Sheba and Seba
    present him gifts.
May all kings bow down to him
    and all nations serve him.

For he will deliver the needy who cry out,
    the afflicted who have no one to help.
He will take pity on the weak and the needy
    and save the needy from death.
He will rescue them from oppression and violence,
    for precious is their blood in his sight.

Long may he live!
    May gold from Sheba be given him.
May people ever pray for him
    and bless him all day long.
May grain abound throughout the land;
    on the tops of the hills may it sway.
May the crops flourish like Lebanon
    and thrive like the grass of the field.
May his name endure forever;
    may it continue as long as the sun.

Then all nations will be blessed through him,
    and they will call him blessed.

Praise be to the LORD God, the God of Israel,
    who alone does marvelous deeds.
Praise be to his glorious name forever;
    may the whole earth be filled with his glory.
                Amen and Amen.

JESUS AND THE KINGDOM

What about Jesus? What was his kingdom message? Flowing directly out of the visionary declarations of Mary, Zechariah, and John, we encounter in Jesus four themes that reveal what he knows God is doing at this crucial (completing) moment in Israel's Story.

First—and perhaps this is the easiest to miss as well as the least interesting because we have heard it before—*Jesus believed the kingdom of God was breaking into history.* Two texts in the Gospels make this abundantly clear. The summary passage of Jesus' preaching according to Mark is: "The time has come.... The kingdom of God *has come near*" (Mark 1:15). The verb in italics (Greek *ēngiken*) does not mean "has arrived" so much as it means "has drawn near," but very near. It describes something more like coming over the crest of a hill where one can see in the distance below one's hometown as one returns home from a journey, or something like seeing the sun's light early in the morning before one can see the orb of the sun. But, still, this term describes something that is very close.

The second text evokes something even closer, so close one has to say, "It is here!" In Matthew 12:28 Jesus says "But if it is by the Spirit of God that I drive out demons, then the kingdom of God *has come upon you.*" Here we find a different Greek word, *ephthasen*, which means "has come upon"; in this instance Jesus clearly believes the experience of exorcism is the actual manifestation of the long-awaited kingdom of God. What Mary, Zechariah, and John said was coming had indeed come.

We dare not miss something here: to speak of the kingdom of God arriving or being near is to evoke a host of images, ideas, and expectations from the Bible on into Jesus' world of Essenes and Sadducees and Pharisees and Zealots. From the promises to Abraham of a land and a people and kings, to God's promise to David for an eternal king and kingdom, right on through the prophetic visions of *shalom* and justice and heartfelt Torah observance, all of this and more, Jesus balled up into the word *kingdom* and said, "Get ready, it's almost here. In fact, in some ways it is already here." For Jesus, "kingdom" carried the weight of his entire eschatology, and he announced that his eschatology was about to turn to the final chapter.

Second, Jesus declares a *new society in the land.* The long-awaited kingdom society will be marked by radical changes, and to express his vision for what God is about to do, Jesus clips lines from Isaiah's

Servant song opening up Isaiah 61 and applies those words to himself in Luke 4:18 – 19:

> The Spirit of the Lord is on me,
>> because he has anointed me
>> to proclaim good news to the poor.
> He has sent me to proclaim freedom for the prisoners
>> and recovery of sight for the blind,
> to set the oppressed free,
>> to proclaim the year of the Lord's favor.

The marked themes for the new society are "good news [gospel]" for the poor, freedom for prisoners, sight for the blind, freedom for the oppressed — and all this as a declaration of the year of the Lord's favor. Clearly, words shaped for the exiles of Isaiah's day and embodied in the "Servant"[54] are taken up by Jesus to apply to himself and for those whom he sees in "exile": the poor, the imprisoned, blind, and the oppressed. All of this is empowered by the Spirit.

Third, Jesus declares *a new citizenship*. The Lukan beatitudes mark off — in a "salvation culture" kind of way — those who are "in" from those who are "out," drawing on a deep theme in the Bible that emerges in its purest form in Deuteronomy 28, the blessings and curses. What Jesus said in his famous sermon shocks and startles because all the "wrong" people are "in" and all the "right" people are "out." What we see here is a radical reversal of the citizens of the kingdom. Luke 6:20 – 26 reads clearly and needs no commentary:

> Looking at his disciples, he said:
>> "Blessed are you who are poor,
>>> for yours is the kingdom of God.
>> Blessed are you who hunger now,
>>> for you will be satisfied.
>> Blessed are you who weep now,
>>> for you will laugh.
>> Blessed are you when people hate you,
>>> when they exclude you and insult you
>>> and reject your name as evil,
>>>> because of the Son of Man.

"Rejoice in that day and leap for joy, because great is your reward in heaven. For that is how their ancestors treated the prophets.

"But woe to you who are rich,
   for you have already received your comfort.
Woe to you who are well fed now,
   for you will go hungry.
Woe to you who laugh now,
   for you will mourn and weep.
Woe to you when everyone speaks well of you,
   for that is how their ancestors treated the false prophets."

Fourth, the wording of the Gospels throws immediate clarity that the kingdom Jesus is announcing is the kingdom *of God*. This kingdom contrasts with that of the Jewish ruler Herod Antipas and the Roman ruler Tiberius. Here we have a radical call by Jesus: he is calling everyone to submit to *God, the God of Israel, YHWH, the Creator and Covenant maker*. The Lord's Prayer of Jesus, which expresses the heart of his vision and mission, begins on this very theme:

Our Father in heaven,
hallowed be your name.
your kingdom come.
your will be done
   on earth as it is in heaven. (Matt. 6:9 – 10)

This implies a personal relationship to God, who is Father, and it implies also God now being the modem from which is given the only signal in the land. Jesus gave to his followers a God-saturated vision of life.

Fifth, and now we come to the center of what gospeling is all about and for some weird reason scholars and preachers alike skip right over the point, Jesus declares *he is at the center of the kingdom of God*. John is in prison; Jesus is free. John commissions two disciples to tell Jesus his condition in the hope that Jesus can do something about the imprisonment. Jesus' response surprises, but it is the closing line that shows Jesus is "gospeling." Luke 7:22 – 23, which clearly draws on Isaiah's great themes of restoration and kingdom in Isaiah 29:18 – 19; 35:5 – 6; and 61:1, reads:

Go back and report to John what you have seen and heard: The blind receive sight, the lame walk, those who have leprosy are cleansed, the deaf hear, the dead are raised, and the good news is proclaimed to the poor. Blessed is anyone who does not stumble on account of me.

Here we need to draw some threads together. What we see is a partial answer to our question: Does Jesus preach the gospel? Or, better yet, does Jesus preach himself as the completion of Israel's Story? To begin with, Mary, Zechariah, and John each focused their theme that Israel's Story was coming to its completion by focusing on a person. To be sure, Zechariah had two persons in mind: John and his successor. But that does not minimize that Mary and Zechariah and John see something that is profoundly *messianic* in how they see the kingdom of God. They each pointed to Jesus as the solution to Israel's yearning.

Even more, *Jesus does the same.* The word for this is *chutzpah* or a robust egocentrism. The startling implications of Luke 4:16–30, the opening preaching scene for Jesus, is that he had the ego to think that Isaiah's words from chapter 61 were finding their way to him as their fulfillment. What must have struck the listeners after hearing him read Isaiah 61's words about the Spirit anointing a "me" to preach the gospel to the poor was this stunning claim: "Today this scripture is fulfilled in your hearing" (4:21). Jesus points at himself even more by responding to anticipated criticisms: "Surely," he says to them, "you will quote this proverb to me," and "Do here in your hometown what we have heard that you did in Capernaum" (4:23). And what does Jesus say next? He speaks of himself in only partially cryptic language: "Truly I tell you ... no prophet is accepted in his hometown" (4:24). And it was in this self-promoting context and it was that egocentrism that led to the villagers to be "furious" and to attempt to put him away right then (4:28–30).

While the theme of self-promotion in the beatitudes is implicit, no one can miss the fact that it was *Jesus* who was saying these things and opening the door for some and shutting it on others. Sure, the attributes of the "in" and the "out" are biblical themes, but it was *Jesus* who was now standing up and telling people who is in the kingdom and who is not. But this all comes to a brilliant completion when Jesus responds to John: Mary, Zechariah, and John combine with Jesus' own words to round off Jesus' words: "Blessed is anyone who does not stumble on account of *me*" (Luke 7:23). That is, Jesus not only believed the kingdom was connected to him and to his mission and teachings, *but he believed the kingdom of God was now breaking into history in himself.* No one ever summed this up more succinctly or more memorably than Origen, that hard-to-classify early Christian theologian, when he said Jesus was not only absolute wisdom, righteousness, and truth, but also "absolute kingdom." The word Origen used for Jesus was that he was *autobasileia*, that is, the "very kingdom itself in person."[55]

Did Jesus preach the gospel when he spoke about kingdom? The question, we are suggesting, is this: Did he preach *himself* as completing Israel's Story when he spoke of kingdom? Anyone who says what Jesus says in Luke 4:16–30 and anyone who sees the themes of Isaiah 28, 35, and 61 in his own miracles and then speaks of being not scandalized about *himself* is clearly promoting himself as God's messianic agent of the kingdom. Yes, he preached the gospel because Jesus preached himself.

Nothing could be clearer about this than our next, usually ignored, set of texts in the Gospels. These texts will form a second way of showing that Jesus preached himself.

WHO AM I? WHO ARE YOU?

There is a set of passages in the Gospels that, if looked at quickly, can both dazzle and be dizzying, but if looked at any quicker than that they can be ignored. Sadly, they are scattered apart enough that many don't even notice them. But if they are looked at more carefully, they lead to delight and the essence of the gospel itself—in fact, studying them together in one setting can make for a profound classroom experience, one I've experienced a number of times.

What we find in these passages is the residue of a number of discussions between John and Jesus. But what is most interesting is that those discussions are concerned with two essential questions each had for the other: "Who am I?" and "Who are you?" More accu-

JESUS AND THE GOSPEL · 101

rately, these two questions are asking one simple question Jesus and John seem to be asking about themselves and one another: "Which figure in the Bible are you now fulfilling?" This question was being asked on local corners of Galilee and all the way into the seats of power in Jerusalem, but the bigger question gets asked in a number of smaller ways, and here are the ones that we will now seek to answer.

Who did others think Jesus was?
Who did others think John was?
Who did John think John was?
Who did John think Jesus was?
Who did Jesus think John was?
Who did Jesus think Jesus was?

There's a winning lottery ticket here because if we can answer these questions, we will be on our way to asking whether Jesus preached the gospel.

We begin with this question: *Who did others think Jesus was?* Jesus himself wondered, so he asked his disciples, and what they answered is found in Matthew 16:14: "Some say John the Baptist; others say Elijah; and still others, Jeremiah or one of the prophets." At the time of Jesus there was a vigorous discussion about who Jesus was, but what strikes the reader who is sensitive to first-century Judaism is that everyone thought Jesus was one of Israel's great prophets (including John himself) come back to life. Clearly, the way to make sense of Jesus was to connect him to one of Israel's prophets.

This, then, leads to a follow-up question: If some of Jesus' contemporaries wondered whether Jesus himself was actually John the Baptist (come back to life), *who did those same others think John was?* This is one of the first questions dealt with in the gospel of John. Some thought John the Baptist was the long-awaited Jewish Messiah, some thought he was Elijah, and others thought he was "the Prophet" (John 1:19–28). What should cause alarms to go off is that John's contemporaries were compelled to make sense of him by finding him written already into the pages of their Bible.

The only way for John's contemporaries to make sense of him

was to see him as one of Israel's prophets come back to life, or even more, perhaps the Messiah himself. But John answered their questions with this: "None of the above." When asked who he was, John could think of no better answer than the figure found in Isaiah 40.

So, *who did John think he was?* John said it clearly: "I am the voice of one calling in the wilderness" (John 1:22–23). John thinks he's the Voice in the Wilderness. John saw his God-ordained and prophecy-directed role in the voice role of Isaiah, and the Voice's job description was to prepare the way for the coming of the Lord.

So much for what people and John thought about John. Though it takes a bit to wind our way through the curves of the gospel stories on these matters, when we get to our destination, which is a bit like arriving for the first time on the Antrim coast of Northern Ireland on a beautiful sunny day, we will discover one of the most gospel-like horizons in the whole Bible.

So we turn now to how contemporaries thought of Jesus. Let's begin with John: *Who did John think Jesus was?* We are all taught to say "Messiah" and move on to more interesting questions, but I think we need to slow down to consider this question a little more carefully. Twice in the Gospels John actually talks about who he thinks Jesus is. In Matthew 3:11–12, with parallels at Mark 1:7–8 and Luke 3:15–18, John says Jesus is the "one who is more powerful than I," and he sees Jesus as the Baptizer-with-Spirit-and-fire. John clearly confesses that Jesus is superior to himself, and it is possible perhaps to connect these terms to "Messiah," but that connection is far from clear.

Furthermore, Luke 7:18–23 contains a discussion in which John asks this "Who are you?" question, and his question reveals that John is still not entirely sure what to think of Jesus. John asks, "Are you the one who is to come, or should we expect someone else?" Commonly this is read more particularly, like this: "Are you the *Messiah?*" The problem with thinking John was really asking if Jesus was the Messiah is that the expression "the one who is coming" is found in the Bible, and it does not (in the Bible) seem to mean "Messiah." This "the one who is coming" expression is found at Malachi 3:1–5 and 4:1–6, and there it does not refer to "Messiah" but to "Elijah."[56]

This is where it gets fun as well as a bit dizzying, but it could appear that John thought Jesus was Elijah. So, when John asked Jesus if he was "the one to come" in Luke 7:19, Jesus' answer was not drawn from Malachi 3 and 4, but instead Jesus drew from Isaiah 29:18 – 19; 35:5 – 6; and 61:1. Which was Jesus' way of saying, "No, John, I am not the Elijah figure in Malachi. I am the one announced in Isaiah." By the way, if the Elijah line of thinking is accurate, it becomes clear that *Jesus disagrees with John over who Jesus is and over who John is!*

But for good reasons not everyone agrees with this Elijah line of thinking. A recent discovery from the Dead Sea Scrolls is convincing more and more that John was asking if Jesus was in fact the Messiah. In a text labeled 4Q521 we find a crystal-clear connection of the word *Messiah* with the expectations that the Messiah will do precisely the things John asked Jesus about. (I've put in italics the words that apply.)

> For the heavens and the earth shall listen to His *Messiah*....
>
> For the Lord attends to the pious and calls the righteous by name. Over the humble His spirit hovers, and He renews the faithful in His strength. For He will honor the pious upon the throne of His eternal kingdom, *setting prisoners free, opening the eyes of the blind, raising up* those who are bowed down....
>
> And the Lord shall do glorious things which have not been done, just as He said. *For He shall heal the critically wounded, He shall revive the dead, He shall send good news to the afflicted, He shall satisfy the poor, He shall guide the uprooted, He shall make the hungry rich.*

Fascinating text, to be sure, and it seems to me to tip the balance back toward the "Messiah."[57] It would take more space than we have to sort this out fully, but thankfully our concern here is not the precise details but the *questions themselves*. In fact, these questions are startling: these two figures, Jesus and John, were both asking identity questions, and both were finding themselves in the pages of the Bible.

If we are a bit mystified by the fragments of the conversation these two had, Jesus de-mystifies it all and brings all into open light.

We begin to find clarity when we ask the next question: *Who did Jesus think John was?* Jesus openly said John was Elijah. You can find this answer in Mark 9:9–13. His disciples ask Jesus this: "Why do the teachers of the law say that Elijah must come first?" Jesus responds:

> To be sure, Elijah does come first, and restores all things. Why then is it written that the Son of Man must suffer much and be rejected? But I tell you, *Elijah* [i.e., John the Baptist] *has come, and they have done to him everything they wished* [decapitation], *just as it is written about him.*

The last few words here remind us of 1 Corinthians 15: "according to the Scriptures." Jesus and John both knew they had a role to play and that role was found in Scripture. John was confused about his role and about Jesus' role, but Jesus was confused about neither: he openly states that John's role is "according to the Scriptures" and he is the "second coming" of Elijah.

This leads us now to the final question, and we've almost arrived on the coastline itself. Just one more hill and we'll be there. *Who did Jesus think Jesus was?* We could take the Luke 7 passage we cited above and say Jesus is the kingdom-bringer and Isaiah-role-completer, or we could put our spoon into the confession of Peter and see Jesus as Messiah, or we could test the waters of different passages, some of which are barely even noticed by Bible readers today. We will use the third method, not so much to arrive at the definitive answer of who Jesus was as to show that Jesus was totally into *preaching himself as the center of God's plan for Israel.* The point I want to make now is fivefold, and it is the heart of the answer to our question whether Jesus himself preached the gospel:

Jesus went to the Bible to define who he was and what his mission was.

Jesus believed he was completing scriptural passages.

Jesus predicted and embraced his death and resurrection.

Jesus therefore preached the gospel *because he preached himself.*

Jesus preached the gospel because he saw himself completing Israel's Story.

A point must be made before we move on. In talking with a world-class New Testament scholar recently, I heard him say this: "The sermons in the book of Acts become thoroughly gospel only from Acts 10 on."

I said, "Why say that?"

He responded: "Because in Acts 10 Peter preaches *about Jesus.* Prior to that, and during the life of Jesus the message was the kingdom of God."

What surprised me about this statement is that it evoked a ghost I thought now long dead, the ghost of Rudolf Bultmann, who famously said that in the early church "the proclaimer [Jesus] became the proclaimed."[58] That ghost was in the habit of whispering that Jesus preached the kingdom, but it was the church that preached Jesus. In other words, the proclaim*er* became the proclaim*ed*, or the one who proclaimed became the Proclaimed One. Yes, one can see why such a claim would become entrenched, and we are required to be careful with what we claim about the Gospels and Jesus and root what we say in the clear texts of the Bible. But, I thought to myself as I sat there, a more careful examination of the Gospels show a *Jesus who unequivocally and without embarrassment nominated himself for Israel's president.*

There's just too much of this "Jesus preaching himself" in the Gospels to ignore or to pass it off as a later layer of the Gospels that has been added as the early Christians (and the Evangelists) reflected about Jesus. Because this has been ignored and because Jesus' preaching of himself is what proves Jesus indeed preached the apostolic gospel, I want to skip through three passages to make this bold and clear, and I do this by way of emphatic repetition of our theme: Jesus is the heart of the gospel Story.

THREE "LOOK AT ME!" PASSAGES
Again, it is fundamentally important if we want to determine if Jesus preached the gospel to examine the pages of the Gospels to see if he preached himself—and if he did so as the one who fulfilled the Story of Israel—and as a saving story. An affirmative answer here leads inevitably to the conclusion that Jesus did indeed preach the

gospel. The question is not about whether Jesus preached justification; the question is about whether he preached the Story of Israel coming to its completion in the story of himself as a saving story. Justification, of course, would follow from that completion as one way to describe how the Jesus of that story saves.

Three passages now that tell us that Jesus is the center of Israel's Story when it comes to moral vision, when it comes to the shape of its leaders, and when it comes to the meaning of his saving death. Because these passages shape everything through the Story of Jesus, we find in them the core of the gospel itself.

PASSAGE 1: HIS MORAL VISION

From locations unexpected and from voices that surprise, not the least of whom would be Gandhi and Tolstoy, Jesus' moral vision is praised, and at the center of that moral vision is the Sermon on the Mount, and at the center of the Sermon on the Mount is a pregnant set of lines that give birth to the entirety of Jesus' kingdom moral vision. Here are Jesus' words, and they show that his behavior and his teachings are *understood as the consummation and completion and resolution and telos point of the Old Testament Law and the Prophets!*

> Do not think that I have come to abolish the Law or the Prophets; I have not come to abolish them *but to fulfill them.* For truly I tell you, until heaven and earth disappear, not the smallest letter, not the least stroke of a pen, will by any means disappear from the Law until everything is accomplished. Therefore anyone who sets aside one of the least of these commands and teaches others accordingly will be called least in the kingdom of heaven, but whoever practices and teaches these commands will be called great in the kingdom of heaven. For I tell you that unless your righteousness surpasses that of the Pharisees and the teachers of the law, you will certainly not enter the kingdom of heaven. (Matt. 5:17 – 20)

Jesus' moral vision was from front to back an Old Testament Story moral vision, but his teachings brought those teachings to their completion. Jesus' words just quoted could mean he was the definitive rabbi or God-inspired revealer or the Messiah of the age to come, or that his teachings clarify and bring to their fullness what needed clarification or fullness in the Law of Moses; but the one thing that is clear is that he sees his teaching in continuity with the Old Testament. And most importantly for our purposes, he sees his teachings as the climactic revelation and resolution of what was yearning for more in the Old Testament.

Perhaps we miss this, too: Jesus sees himself as the one who speaks the mind of God, and the antitheses of Matthew 5:21 – 48 ("you have heard ... but I say") without doubt reveal his speaking for God in a new day. No small claim! From this point on, Jesus claims, everyone's moral life is to be measured by whether they live according to his moral vision.

PASSAGE 2: JESUS AND THE TWELVE

Jesus chose twelve, not ten and not fifty, disciples. There is a reason for selecting "twelve," and the more one ponders what he was doing, the more one is convinced that Jesus definitely intended to make a public, yea cosmic, statement about the Story of Israel and how his own story was to be fitted into Israel's Story. Nearly everyone at the time of Jesus believed that part of the Jewish hope was for the twelve tribes to be reunited when God wrapped up his plans and sent the Messiah. Judah and Israel would once again be the Twelve-Tribe People of God. One finds this, for instance, in Zechariah 11 and in *Psalms of Solomon* 17:50.

But this eschatological hope dimension of "twelve" is not enough. More central to the term *twelve* is the covenant God made with Israel. Over and over in the Old Testament *twelve* means the covenant people of God in their fullness or in their totality. One is not far from the truth in saying that *twelve* is an *ecclesial* (or church) term more than it is a prophetic or an eschatological term.

So, when Jesus chooses twelve (Mark 6:7 – 13) and when he promises the twelve will sit on the twelve thrones (Matt. 19:28), Jesus evokes both Israel's prophetic expectation and the fullness of God's covenant people. But what might be missed is this, and I think missing this is a colossal failure: *Jesus does not include himself in the twelve.* He's not one of them. He's above them. He is the Lord or King (or Messiah!) over the twelve, not just one of the twelve.

All in all, then, Jesus chooses twelve to embody the hope for a reunited twelve tribes; he sees the twelve as embodying the fullness of the people of God, and he sees himself above the twelve.[59] Let's get back to our theme of Jesus and the gospel with this claim: in the act of choosing twelve, Jesus is "preaching the gospel" because in that very action he sees the Story of Israel coming to its completion in the twelve apostles, and he sees himself both as appointer of the twelve and the Lord over the twelve.

PASSAGE 3: JESUS AND HIS DEATH

There is a long and conflicted history of scholarship when it comes to knowing just what Jesus knew about his death and what he didn't know. I have myself weighed in on this debate in a heavy book called *Jesus and His Death*.[60] Suffice it to say that, even though I believe the historical method runs out of gas before it reaches its goal, a responsible historical method can reasonably conclude that Jesus not only anticipated his death but also *interpreted it*. What matters most for this study is that Jesus not only discerned a premature death—how could he not have with John's head rolling around on a platter?—but that he had a reflexive need to explain his inevitable and impending death through Israel's own Scriptures. I want to point to two of those Scriptures now.

In Mark 9:31 Jesus utters these words, and many think this is the most primitive and original of Jesus' passion predictions: "The Son of Man is going to be delivered over into the hands of men. They will kill him, and after three days he will rise."

Jesus captures his fate—and notice this—by connecting his fate with the "Son of Man," that famous figure found in Daniel 7. All I wish to draw our attention to in this context is that *Jesus explained his fate—a death and resurrection—by appealing to Scripture*. But he didn't just prove something from the Bible. *He saw himself in the Son of Man figure who suffered and was exalted*. Does it not occur to you at times what you would think of someone who did this today? Doing this sort of thing inevitably leads to this question, as it did at the time of Jesus: "Who do you think you are?"

Following a triumphal entry into Jerusalem on a donkey, which was simultaneously a mockery of the Roman military's arrogant posture in taking over a city and a staged enactment of the prophet Zechariah's royal entry, Jesus protests in the temple and then, a few nights later, "stages" a Passover-like meal during which time he declares his body and blood will liberate (Mark 14:12–26). As God protected the children of Israel at Passover because they had blood on the door as God's covenant people, so God will protect the followers of Jesus if they will drink of his blood-cup and eat his body-bread. God will, in effect, see the blood on their heart's door and will protect and liberate his followers from Rome and oppression. Once again, the Story of Israel—in particular the Passover Story of Israel—comes to completion in the Story of Jesus; *what must be observed is that Jesus is the one who tells us this. He is self-testifying of his centrality in the Story of Israel coming to completion.*

ONE MORE EXAMPLE

If you have any questions now about whether or not Jesus saw himself as the saving completion of Israel's Story and, therefore, "gospeled the gospel," I will simply quote a story from Luke 24 that reveals how gospel-shaped Jesus was. The story is when Jesus, after his resurrection, explained to disciples the meaning of the entire Story of Israel as it finally came to resolution in himself.

Here's the setting:

> Now that same day two of them were going to a village called Emmaus, about seven miles from Jerusalem. They were talking with each other about everything that had happened. As they talked and discussed these things with each other, Jesus himself came up and walked along with them; but they were kept from recognizing him. (24:13–16)

Question, response, question, response:

> He asked them, "What are you discussing together as you walk along?"
> They stood still, their faces downcast. One of them, named Cleopas, asked him, "Are you the only one visiting Jerusalem who does not know the things that have happened there in these days?"
> "What things?" he asked.
> "About Jesus of Nazareth," they replied. "He was a prophet,

110 · THE KING JESUS GOSPEL

powerful in word and deed before God and all the people. The chief priests and our rulers handed him over to be sentenced to death, and they crucified him; but we had hoped that he was the one who was going to redeem Israel. And what is more, it is the third day since all this took place. In addition, some of our women amazed us. They went to the tomb early this morning but didn't find his body. They came and told us that they had seen a vision of angels, who said he was alive. Then some of our companions went to the tomb and found it just as the women had said, but they did not see Jesus." (24:17–24)

Jesus teaches them how to read the Bible in gospel fashion:

He said to them, "How foolish you are, and how slow to believe all that the prophets have spoken! Did not the Messiah have to suffer these things and then enter his glory?" And beginning with Moses and all the Prophets, he explained to them what was said in all the Scriptures concerning himself. (24:25–27)

Question: How did they respond? We don't know, but we do know this:

As they approached the village to which they were going, Jesus continued on as if he were going farther. But they urged him strongly, "Stay with us, for it is nearly evening; the day is almost over." So he went in to stay with them. (24:28–29)

Recognition comes at the table, as at the Last Supper:

When he was at the table with them, he took bread, gave thanks, broke it and began to give it to them. Then their eyes were opened and they recognized him, and he disappeared from their sight. They asked each other, "Were not our hearts burning within us while he talked with us on the road and opened the Scriptures to us?" (24:30–32)

Witness to Jesus:

They got up and returned at once to Jerusalem. There they found the Eleven and those with them, assembled together and saying, "It is true! The Lord has risen and has appeared to Simon." Then the two told what had happened on the way, and how Jesus was recognized by them when he broke the bread. (24:33–35)

Jesus brings peace to those who see him as the gospel itself:

> While they were still talking about this, Jesus himself stood among them and said to them, "Peace be with you." (24:36)

We've now looked at what I'm calling the "Look at Me!" passages. When Jesus talks about moral vision, he sees himself completing the Torah and the Prophets. When he summons the twelve to be his apostles, he is summing up Israel's hope and Israel's covenant community as its Lord. And when Jesus speaks about his premature death, he sees it as fulfilling Scriptures, not the least of which is the defining event: Passover itself. And I have not dipped into other "I have come" passages, like Matthew 9:13 and 10:34–35, and we have barely touched on Jesus' incredibly self-centered claim that the Son of Man figure of Daniel 7 mirrors his own ministry and destiny in so many ways. But already we have established enough to say that John 14:6's claim is a dead ringer for who Jesus thought he was: "I am the way and the truth and the life."

So we are back to our question, a question now made much more clear.

CONCLUSION

Did Jesus preach the gospel? Yes, he preached the gospel because the gospel is the saving Story of Jesus completing Israel's Story, and Jesus clearly set himself at the center of God's saving plan for Israel. I agree with my friend and colleague Klyne Snodgrass, who said Jesus "was not just part of his own good news but the key factor in what was happening."[61] The Gospels, by their very nature, tell a Story of Jesus on center stage on every page. The Gospels are the gospel and Jesus preached the gospel. Again, Pope Benedict XVI gets this precisely right: "There is, then, no discontinuity between Jesus' pre-Easter message and the message preached by the disciples after Easter and Pentecost."[62] Why? Because Jesus preached Jesus and Paul preached Jesus and Peter preached Jesus. Preaching Jesus is preaching the gospel.

In fact, Jesus almost says he and the gospel are one and the same. Listen to this word of Jesus from Mark 8:35: "For whoever wants to save their life will lose it, but whoever loses their life *for me* and *for the gospel* will save it." In this text "for me [my sake]" and "for the [sake of the] gospel" are brought into the closest relationship possible. To respond to Jesus was to respond to the gospel; to respond to the gospel was to respond to Jesus.

But this leads to what will be perhaps my most provocative question: Evangelism, what is it? To "evangelize" or to "gospel" is to tell the Story of Jesus as a saving story that completes Israel's Story. What is the best way to evangelize today? Is it to use the Plan of Salvation and frame it in a Method of Persuasion? We are driven to ask how the apostles evangelized. The book of Acts has seven summaries of evangelistic sermons. What do we learn?

CHAPTER 8

THE GOSPEL OF PETER

JESUS PREACHED THE GOSPEL. The Gospels tell us the gospel. Paul passed on the apostolic gospel tradition. Each of these three has the same gospel, the declaration that the yearning in the Story of Israel finds a satisfactory resolution in the forgiving Story of Jesus. Three stable legs propping up the gospel chair in which we rest.

But, we need a fourth. I don't know if you've ever sat on a chair with three stable legs on either one absent leg or one weak leg, but I have. It can be done but you need to be conscious lest you somehow shift your weight to the wrong leg and find yourself tumbling backward with your limbs flying akimbo. I know that from experience too. In fact, one of the chairs I sat on in a class one semester had a weak fourth leg ... and when I got excited or had to hop up to draw something on the board, it was not unusual to experience the thrill of a chair about to tip over if I didn't steady myself but quick.

For some odd reason the fourth leg for our gospel chair is an ignored leg, as if someone taught us long ago how to sit on a three-legged chair. We've learned to do it so well we don't even know there's a fourth. This chapter will put that fourth leg back in place and ask us all to sit back now with full assurance that we sit on a chair with full supports. That fourth leg is the gospel preaching of the apostles in the book of Acts. We'll let Peter's gospel preaching be the leg since we've already looked at Paul.

But because Paul also has gospel sermons in the book of Acts, we will pause at times to listen to how Paul stands in support of the gospel preaching of Peter. Instead of trotting out all the verses and so make the obvious points of connection between Peter and Paul tedious, I will quote my own doctoral supervisor, Jimmy Dunn, one of the world's leading authorities on Paul: in Acts "Paul preaches the same message as Peter."[63] To be sure, there are differences between their sermons, but it does not take but a second reading of the sermons in Acts to see that these two great apostles were standing together for the one apostolic gospel.

TWO ELEPHANTS IN THE ROOM

We want to know what the first gospel was really like. We want to know how that first generation of apostles evangelized, and we want to know how that early gospeling compares to what we call evangelism and the gospel today. Time and time again, and I can't explain this, our discussions of gospeling simply ignore those gospeling sermons in the book of Acts. It's as if there is a big elephant or two in the room and we are doing our best to ignore them. It is standing in the way and keeping us from seeing our final supporting leg for understanding the apostolic gospel. Would there be—correct that, *could* there be—any better source for evangelism than a half dozen or so gospel sermon summaries from the first generation of the apostles?

I make two observations on which I will not give an inch: first, *there are seven or eight gospel sermons or summaries of gospel sermons in the book of Acts.* Here they are (and you can find them in appendix 3):

Acts 2:14–39
Acts 3:12–26
Acts 4:8–12
Acts 10:34–43, with 11:4–18
Acts 13:16–41
Acts 14:15–17
Acts 17:22–31
(Acts 7:2–53)

If we count Stephen's sermon in Acts 7, we have eight. If we don't, we have seven. These seven (or eight) sermons are pristine, first-generation gospel sermons. If we have any Protestant bones in our body, we want to know what they gospeled and how they gospeled, and we want our gospeling to be rooted in and conformed to this gospeling. They are right there raising their hands to get our attention, and I want to give them the attention they deserve.

First Corinthians 15 outlines the gospel but doesn't "gospel" in a public setting. It simply tells us what the gospel is. The Gospels are not evangelistic sermons but they are indeed the gospel. But what we've got in the book of Acts are more or less summaries of the gospeling of the apostles Peter and Paul, and perhaps Stephen. Now that I've brought in Stephen, just one word: I'm going to ignore Stephen's sermon because, while it completely conforms to Peter's and Paul's sermons in that it declares boldly the Story of Israel coming to resolution in Jesus, the ending of the sermon is not a call to repent, believe, and be baptized but a finger-pointing exercise of apologetics and condemnation. There is gospeling in this sermon, but it is better classified as apologetics and prophetic warning. Nothing substantial will be lost by ignoring it.

Now for my second observation: these seven summaries of sermons in the book of Acts are *gospeling* sermons. They are, in effect, instances of first-century evangelism. I will avoid commenting on each, but here is a fulsome list of instances in Acts that show that the sermons, preaching, and teaching of Jesus, Peter, Paul, and others were acts of gospeling:

- Acts 2:40–41: With many other words he warned them; and he pleaded with them, "Save yourselves from this corrupt generation." Those who accepted *his message* were baptized, and about three thousand were added to their number that day.
- 5:42: Day after day, in the temple courts and from house to house, they never stopped teaching and *proclaiming the good news* that Jesus is the Messiah.
- 10:36: You know the *message* God sent to the people of Israel, announcing the *good news* of peace through Jesus Christ, who is Lord of all.
- 10:42: He commanded us to *preach* to the people and to testify that he is the one whom God appointed as judge of the living and the dead.

- 13:5: When they arrived at Salamis, they *proclaimed the word of God* in the Jewish synagogues. John was with them as their helper.
- 13:7b: The proconsul, an intelligent man, sent for Barnabas and Saul because he wanted to *hear the word of God.*
- 13:15: After the reading from the Law and the Prophets, the leaders of the synagogue sent word to them, saying, "Brothers, if you have *a word of exhortation* for the people, please speak."
- 13:26: "Fellow children of Abraham and you God-fearing Gentiles, it is to us that *this message of salvation* has been sent."
- 13:32: We tell you the *good news*: What God promised our ancestors...
- 14:7: ... where they continued to *preach the gospel.*
- 14:21: They *preached the gospel* in that city and won a large number of disciples.
- 16:10: After Paul had seen the vision, we got ready at once to leave for Macedonia, concluding that God had called us to *preach the gospel* to them.
- 17:18: A group of Epicurean and Stoic philosophers began to debate with him. Some of them asked, "What is this babbler trying to say?" Others remarked, "He seems to be advocating foreign gods." They said this because Paul was *preaching the good news about Jesus and the resurrection.*
- 28:31: He *proclaimed* the kingdom of God and taught about the Lord Jesus Christ—with all boldness and without hindrance!

These two observations lead me to say of these two elephants in the room that if we ignore these passages, we will make two colossal mistakes: we will both fail to see *what* the gospel was and we will fail to see *how* the apostles gospeled. The book of Acts, even when the passage does not begin with a road sign that says "Apostolic Evangelism Ahead," frames the entire twenty-eight chapters in a story of apostolic gospeling from Jerusalem to Rome.

Here is what we see.

ISRAEL'S STORY FRAMED THE
GOSPEL OF THE APOSTLES

The apostles were not like our modern soterians because they did not empty the gospel of its Story, nor did they reduce the gospel to the Plan of Salvation. In fact, the apostles were the original, robust evangelicals. It all has to do with how the gospel is framed. Peter and Paul framed their gospeling through the grid of Israel's Story coming to its destination in the Story of Jesus. Neither did they frame their gospel from the perspective of an atonement theory—whether the ransom theory or the penal substitution theory. Salvation and atonement flow out of the gospel, and Paul can call his gospel the "message of salvation" (13:26), but neither atonement nor salvation was how the apostles framed the gospel.

From Peter's world-transforming sermon in Acts 2 to Paul's sermon on the Areopagus in Acts 17, it was the Story of Israel that shaped how they gospeled. If we want to get "gospel" right, we will need to remember that in the heart of that apostolic gospel tradition in 1 Corinthians 15 is "according to the Scriptures." As we will discuss in this chapter, the sermons in the book of Acts put muscle *and fat* on that very "according to the Scriptures" bone in the apostolic gospel tradition.

What, then, did "according to the Scriptures" look like when they preached? In Peter's first gospel sermon, as sketched in Acts 2:13–21, he quotes Joel 2:28–32 and Psalm 16:8–11 and 110:1. (Again, you can read Peter's sermons in Appendix 3.) Peter journeys backward in time into the depths of Israel's Story so he can show that the whole story points forward to Jesus Christ and Pentecost. Peter's depth of insight and the dexterity of his memory in Acts 2 reveal what might be the single most significant theological shift among the apostles: Jesus' resurrection and the profound experience with the Holy Spirit at Pentecost led the apostles into a "hermeneutical revolution." They suddenly had new eyes to reread and reinterpret the Old Testament from the perspective of the Story of Jesus. We need to remind ourselves constantly that the apostles, who all gospeled like this, didn't have iPads, iPods, or iPhones with a Bible search engine that could chase down a favorite word in the Bible. The apostles had memory.

and that memory was reconfigured by the Story of Jesus so much that their way of reading the Bible was transformed.

In his second gospel sermon, found in Acts 3:22–23, Peter quotes Deuteronomy 18:15, 18–19, that famous passage in the Old Testament about the future prophet-like-Moses. Jesus is that prophet according to Peter's gospel. At Acts 3:25 Peter quotes Genesis 22:18 or 26:4—both mentioning the blessing of Gentiles—to establish the Abrahamic origins of the gospel.[64] In Acts 10:43 Peter finishes off the gospeling event at Cornelius's house by making a claim that only folks as far removed as we are can miss its extravagance: "*All* the prophets testify about" Jesus Christ.

Like Peter, the apostle Paul in his famous and most complete evangelistic sermon, found at Acts 13:16–41, begins with these words: "Fellow Israelites and you Gentiles who worship God, listen to me! The God of the people of Israel chose our ancestors" (13:16–17), and he proceeds straight through Israel's history until he gets to Jesus with these words: "From this man's [David's] descendants God has brought to Israel the Savior Jesus, as he promised" (13:23). Not many words later Paul summarizes his message with this: "We tell you the good news: What God promised our ancestors he has fulfilled for us, their children, by raising up Jesus" (13:32–33). That is the framing story of the gospel for the apostles. This framing story is so pervasive that we fail the apostolic gospel tradition if we fail to make it our framing gospel story.

These citations of Scripture aren't apologetic props in a sermon that could get by without those props. No, the apostles' gospel was the Story of Jesus resolving the Story of Israel. The texts the apostles quoted from the Old Testament weren't props; they were the light posts to help Israel find its way from Abraham to Jesus.

As I wrote the paragraphs above, I was also thinking of how often this way of reading the whole Bible toward Christ happens in other places in the New Testament, so much so that we have to say that the Story of Jesus led to a "conversion of their imagination."[65] Like this one from Peter in 1 Peter 1:10–12:

> Concerning this salvation, the prophets, who spoke of the grace that was to come to you, searched intently and with the greatest

care, trying to find out the time and circumstances to which the Spirit of Christ in them was pointing when he predicted the sufferings of the Messiah and the glories that would follow. It was revealed to them that they were not serving themselves but you, when they spoke of the things that have now been told you by those who have preached the gospel to you by the Holy Spirit sent from heaven. Even angels long to look into these things.

Or this one from Hebrews 1:1–4:

In the past God spoke to our ancestors through the prophets at many times and in various ways, but in these last days he has spoken to us by his Son, whom he appointed heir of all things, and through whom also he made the universe. The Son is the radiance of God's glory and the exact representation of his being, sustaining all things by his powerful word. After he had provided purification for sins, he sat down at the right hand of the Majesty in heaven. So he became as much superior to the angels as the name he has inherited is superior to theirs.

What the prophets were yearning for in images that they themselves ached to comprehend and what they were glimpsing in all but fully comprehensible ways suddenly appeared one day in the land of Israel, and his name was Yeshua ben Yoseph and Miriam. Once they encountered him, their Bible became a new book *precisely because they read it as gospel.*

Back to Peter's gospeling.

THE APOSTLES DECLARE THE WHOLE STORY OF JESUS AS GOSPEL

Peter's gospeling also puts the life of a live body on the bones of 1 Corinthians 15, and that means his gospel involved telling the full Story of Jesus Christ, including his life, his death, his resurrection, his exaltation, the gift of the Holy Spirit, his second coming, and the wrapping up of history so that God would be all in all. The reason we have to say this is because too often we have...

reduced the life of Jesus to Good Friday, and therefore reduced the gospel to the crucifixion, and then soterians have reduced Jesus to transactions of a Savior.

Not so in the early gospeling, for in those early apostolic sermons, we see the whole life of Jesus. In fact, if they gave an emphasis to one dimension of the life of Jesus, it was the resurrection. The apostolic gospel could not have been signified or painted or sketched with a crucifix. That gospel wanted expression as an empty cross because of the empty tomb. The clearest example of Peter's whole-life-of-Jesus with an emphasis on cross-leading-to-resurrection gospel is seen at Acts 10:36–42, and I would urge you to read this entirely and slowly:

> You know the message God sent to the people of Israel, announcing the good news [gospel] of peace through Jesus Christ, who is Lord of all.

> That message spread throughout Judea, beginning in Galilee after the baptism that John announced:

> How God anointed Jesus of Nazareth with the Holy Spirit and power, and how he went around doing good and healing all who were under the power of the devil, because God was with him.
>
> We are witnesses to all that he did in the country of the Jews and in Jerusalem. They killed him by hanging him on a cross, but God raised him from the dead on the third day and caused him to be seen. He was not seen by all the people, but by witnesses whom God had already chosen — by us who ate and drank with him after he rose from the dead. He commanded us to preach to the people and to testify that he is the one whom God appointed as judge of the living and the dead.

This text is not quite complete, but if one adds together what we find in Acts 2:22–35; 3:13–15, 19–21; and 10:37–42, we discover that Peter preached the whole Story of Jesus as Messiah.[66] Let's remind ourselves once again that these sermons in Acts are apostolic evangelistic sermons. The gospel itself they declared looked like the text we just quoted, and some today preach that same gospel.

PASTOR FLEMING

Pastor Fleming Rutledge is considered one of America's best preachers. She's a bestselling author who devoted years of her preaching ministry to the book of Romans and its unlocking of the mysteries of sin and death through the gospel. When she preaches, and there's a collection of her sermons on Romans called *Not Ashamed of the Gospel,*[67] she has an apostolic emphasis on the cross and the resurrection—and she appeals time and time again to the wider Story of Jesus in his life and teachings as she opens up the grandeur of Romans. Hear, then, these words about redemption in the events of Jesus' life that sum up his entire ministry:

> But we must remember there is only way that we can participate in Christ's victory over the demonic Powers. We can only do it by doing it his way. If we try to do it our way we will be back into the rule of Sin and Death. The only way of victory is through the Cross.

And she zeroes in on the power of the gospel for today:

> Young people today are faced with so many pressures to assume so many "lifestyles." The messages are all essentially the same ... and your lifestyle will be limitless.
>
> It's a lie. All of it is a lie. None of these things can give life. The sign of Sin and Death lies across them all. But there is news today. I am among you as a fellow prisoner who brings news of impending release. *The first man, Adam, is strong; but the second man, Christ, is stronger still.*

There it is: Jesus died with us and instead of us and for us, but that same God raised Jesus from the dead, and that resurrection unleashes the power of the Stronger Man to those who will enter that Story of Jesus. The Stronger Man brings victory through his death and resurrection.

Pastor Fleming's sermons, including one called "The Remaking of the World," kept driving me back to 1 Corinthians 15. But Pastor Fleming's gospel and Peter's gospel involve King Jesus' exaltation. This leads to Pentecost and the Spirit's empowering presence in the earliest churches and today.[68] Notice that it is the exalted Jesus who is qualified to send the Spirit (2:33). From Acts 1:8 on, the Spirit shapes everything important, and so I want to pile on some scriptural texts to make this abundantly clear: Jesus had the Holy Spirit

(10:38) and then dispersed the Holy Spirit to the church. This Spirit of Pentecost is distributed to all (2:1 – 4), the Spirit endowed prophesies and visions and dreams (2:17 – 18; 11:28; 13:4; 21:11), and the repentant believer receives the Spirit along with forgiveness of sins (2:38; 5:32; 8:15 – 17; 10:44 – 47).

Scan through Acts to observe the effects of the apostolic gospel: "After they prayed, the place where they were meeting was shaken. And they were all filled with the Holy Spirit and spoke the word of God boldly" (Acts 4:31; cf. 6:10; 7:55; 13:4, 9; see also 16:6 – 7; 19:6).

THE APOSTLES SUMMED UP THE
GOSPEL IN WORDS ABOUT JESUS

I live and dwell among scholars who examine the Gospels to discern what Jesus was really like, and we've got all kinds of "Jesuses" in our world: the social activist, the prophet, the miracle worker, the religious genius, the social contrarian, the Republican and the Democrat and the Marxist Jesus, and the anti-empire Jesus ... I could go on. But if we want to hear afresh that original gospel, we need to ask what labels the apostles used for Jesus. What were the terms and titles for Jesus that Peter and the apostles used when they gospeled? The answer to this one is foundational if we want to understand the apostolic gospel.

Peter made stupendous claims about Jesus; either they are true or they are ridiculous because they are that stupendous. Peter's Jesus of Nazareth, the one who lived and died and who was raised and ascended and enthroned, is both *Messiah of Israel and Lord of the whole world*. Those are the terms of the early gospeling in the book of Acts, and if we want to be faithful to the Bible, those should be our terms as well. Those titles for Jesus tell the gospel Story of Jesus. Thus, Acts 2:36:

> Therefore let all Israel be assured of this: *God has made this Jesus, whom you crucified, both Lord and Messiah.*

And in Acts 10:34 – 38, where Peter justifies gospeling *Gentiles* like Cornelius, we read:

> I now realize how true it is that God does not show favoritism but accepts from every nation the one who fears him and does what

is right. You know the message God sent to the people of Israel, announcing the good news of peace through Jesus Christ, who is *Lord of all*. You know what has happened throughout the province of Judea, beginning in Galilee after the baptism that John preached — how God *anointed* Jesus of Nazareth with the Holy Spirit and power, and how he went around doing good and healing all who were under the power of the devil, because God was with him.

Peter reads a Bible that leads him to see God at work guiding the Story of Israel into the Story of Jesus, and the Jesus of that story is Israel's true King and the Lord over all (cf. also 2:39; 3:25–26; 10:44–47; 11:16–18). Peter knows this because God raised Jesus from the grave. There are other terms Peter uses for Jesus, including "servant" (3:13), "the Holy and Righteous One" (3:14), "the author of life" (3:15), and the "prophet" (3:22–23), but these supplement his two major terms, "Messiah" and "Lord." All the apostles saw Jesus as Messiah and Lord, and all you have to do is open your Bible to any of the New Testament letters and these terms jump off the page. For the apostles, it was all about King Jesus.

I appreciate the work of historians who shed light on Jesus, but those who are faithful to the apostolic gospel have a set of terms that defines who Jesus was, is, and will be, what Jesus did, and how we are to approach him: Jesus is Messiah and Lord, and as Messiah and Lord he is Savior, Son of God, and Servant. Perhaps we need to remind ourselves again that these terms are drawn from the Story of Israel, but they are more than clever titles; the use of these terms *interprets* the entire story in a way that recasts the whole. By using these terms (and not Latin terms like *dominus* or *Caesar*), the apostles were saying that the story they were telling of Jesus was the old, old Story of Israel now coming to its resolution point in Jesus because he was the true King of Israel.

Let this be said over and over: the apostolic gospel was framed in such a way that the story *was centered on and revolved around Jesus*. To gospel was (and is) to declare the royal truth about King Jesus. Jesus was (and is) the gospel. In this chapter we focus on Peter, but there is something about Paul's gospeling in Acts that deserves our attention before we return to Peter's own preaching.

THE APOSTLE PAUL PAVES NEW GROUND
BY ADAPTING GOSPEL TO AUDIENCE

The apostle Paul was the "apostle to the Gentiles" while Peter was the "apostle to the Jews." Aren't there differences in the way these two apostles preach the gospel? Did they declare the same gospel and same story to Gentiles that they did to Jews? Surely there's got to be some room for variation and variant gospel shapings. There is. Plenty. And Paul is the one in whom we see those adaptations. This great apostle to the Gentiles had discovered God's gospel plan included Gentiles, and so he was pushing the gospel into the Gentile world nonstop. If you take someone like Paul, who had a quick mind and a yearning to persuade, and if you set him up to gospel in any of the major cities on the Mediterranean (say philosophically minded Athens or pride-drenched Rome), his words will morph into a message intelligible and challenging to his specific audience.

Let's begin in one of the smaller cities in which Paul preached, in Asia Minor's Lystra. After a miraculous healing, the Lystrans were about to turn the messengers into gods:

> The crowd ... shouted in the Lycaonian language, "The gods have come down to us in human form!" Barnabas they called Zeus, and Paul they called Hermes because he was the chief speaker. The priest of Zeus, whose temple was just outside the city, brought bulls and wreaths to the city gates because he and the crowd wanted to offer sacrifices to them. (Acts 14:11–13)

This turn of events is almost comic for readers today, but not in Paul's Roman world. Seeing what they were about to do, which any devout Jew would have immediately recognized as idolatrous and blasphemous, Paul finds a way to turn off their idolatrous instincts. Paul now shapes his gospel message to the context by digging into some natural revelation and some old-fashioned common sense. But what we need to see here is that idol worship is a natural target for Paul's gospel *because it concerned the godness of God and the lordship of King Jesus.*

> Friends, why are you doing this? We too are only human, like you. We are bringing you good news, telling you to turn from

these worthless things to the living God, who made the heavens and the earth and the sea and everything in them. In the past, he let all nations go their own way. Yet he has not left himself without testimony: He has shown kindness by giving you rain from heaven and crops in their seasons; he provides you with plenty of food and fills your hearts with joy. (Acts 14:15–17)[69]

Regardless of his ability to adapt to context, that Gentile audience did not stop Paul from seeing the sweep of history through the scriptural Story of Israel that found its completion in the Story of Jesus. The summary at Lystra draws deeply from the creation story, that the one true God is the Creator and humans are not to step into that sacred space. Adam and Eve tried that; the folks who built the Tower of Babel tried that; the pagans have been doing that forever and a day, but the gospel cuts into any breaching of that sacred space: God alone is God.

On the Areopagus and in the premier city of Greek renown, Athens, where Paul was clearly gospeling to Gentiles who had no knowledge of Israel's Scriptures, he was surely tempted to be at his intellectual best. He was, but that didn't stop him from setting the stage for Jesus by sketching Israel's history — minus the election and covenant stuff. He observed their useless idols, assumed they were yearning for a robust monotheism, and then told that Gentile audience that in fact Israel's one and only God is the Creator. Here Paul was no doubt appealing to Genesis 1–2. Furthermore, in the face of shrines and temples and idols in the most public of places, the apostle to the Gentiles declared boldly that this one and only God of Israel does not dwell in physical structures. Further, he appealed again to Israel's Story of Adam and the unity of all humans, saying: "from one man [Adam, with Eve assumed] [God] made all the nations, that they should inhabit the whole earth" (Acts 17:26). Paul drew from the well of his one and only story: Israel's Story. That story was deeply shaped by the utter sacredness of the lordship of God.

To be sure, Paul adapts the gospel to his audience in many ways, and I'll point to two instances. Paul first focuses on *what Gentiles and Jews have in common.* God is the invisible Creator of all of creation, which means God is common to all religions (Acts 17:24–30).

What is also in common can be called an "inner apologetic." By this I mean that there is something in each human being that reaches out for God, and that reaching instinct comes from God and leads to God. Paul discerns this aching for deity in the idols around Athens, especially the one "To an unknown god" (17:23). Thus, Acts 17:27–28 has some lines that begin (most likely) with a quotation from Epimenides and conclude with a quotation from the third-century BC poet Aratus:

> God did this so that they would seek him and perhaps reach out for him and find him, though he is not far from any one of us. "For in him we live and move and have our being." As some of your own poets have said, "We are his offspring."

I feel some of Paul's anguish. My own travel to the ruins in both Pompei on the Amalfi coast and to Ostia Antica, Rome's first-century port, impressed on me the constant presence of altars, shrines, temples, and overt religiosity. That overwhelming presence of idols was a threat to both Jewish and Christian monotheism and called forth constant reactions and criticisms in the Jewish literature. We must, however, remind ourselves that because the gospel itself declares that King Jesus is the true Lord over all, gospeling meant focusing on the false gods and idolatries of his Roman listeners.

A second example of adaptation is that *Paul does not speak directly either of Jesus Christ or of the crucifixion of Jesus Christ when he is on the Areopagus.* What Paul does say about Jesus needs to be quoted:

> In the past God overlooked such ignorance, but now he commands all people everywhere to repent. For he has set a day when he will judge the world with justice *by the man he has appointed. He has given proof of this to everyone by raising him from the dead.* (Acts 17:30–31)

Paul's audience surely didn't know enough of Israel's Story to know what to make of this Jewish Jesus. So Paul starts where they are. The apostle permits the entire weight of the gospel message to be hoisted onto the back of the resurrection of this one man, Jesus Christ, as an act of the one God. But bringing up resurrection is hardly an act of adaptation. It needs to be observed that Paul's notion of "resurrection" is not adapted into the terms of the Platonic belief in the "immortality of the soul," and N. T. Wright's book *The Resurrection of the Son of God* makes this point over and over.[70] Resurrection as "life after life after death" is not the same thing as the immortal soul carrying on after it escapes from the body. What Paul says about resurrection was not a touchstone with the Athenians; it was a sharp-edged difference. This gospeling Jew jabbed them where they were most confident, and he rested his gospel on that one difference.

I have perhaps slightly overstated this element of resurrection. The actual weight of Paul's gospeling on the Areopagus is even better carried in true gospel fashion by Paul's *Christology*. Paul's words are that God will someday judge the whole world "by *the man* [God] has appointed" (Acts 17:31). When we are done imaginatively listening to Paul on the Areopagus, the first question many, if not most, of his pagan listeners would have asked was, "Who is this Jesus?" Or, "Who is this man? Why is he the judge of all? Why was he raised from the dead?" Precisely the sorts of gospel questions Jesus generated in his own life. True gospeling that conforms to the apostolic gospel leads directly to who Jesus is, whatever the gospeler has to say to get folks to move in that direction. Once there, the apostolic gospeling in the book of Acts summons the audience to respond.

THE APOSTLES SUMMONED PEOPLE TO RESPOND
The apostolic gospeling in the book of Acts forms a powerful support for what gospeling can be today. One of the most important contributions that Acts makes to gospeling is the *how*—for it is in these sermons that we see how the apostles called people to respond. And they are consistent: to participate in the Story of Jesus the apostles called people *to believe, to repent,* and *to be baptized*.[71] I would contend that there is no such thing as gospeling that does not include the summons to respond in faith, repentance, and baptism.

A good example of this process is Peter's summons to the people to *believe* in Acts 10–11, and the word here means to "trust one's entire person and salvation to" Jesus Christ.[72] Note these two verses:

> All the prophets testify about him that everyone who *believes* in
> him receives forgiveness of sins through his name. (Acts 10:43)

So if God gave them the same gift he gave us who *believed* in the Lord Jesus Christ, who was I to think that I could stand in God's way? (11:17)

And Paul calls for the same response at 13:38 – 39:

Therefore, my friends, I want you to know that through Jesus the forgiveness of sins is proclaimed to you. Through him everyone who *believes* is set free from every sin, a justification you were not able to obtain under the law of Moses.

To believe means more than just mentally agreeing to some truth, even if that truth is that Jesus is Messiah and Lord over all. The entire sweep of the Story of Israel and the Story of Jesus ushers us into a world where God's people rely on and trust in God, and such a trusting relationship generates a life of obedience, holiness, and love. Our relationship with God is depicted by Hosea in the terms of a marriage, and just as a husband and wife are not only absent of infidelities but also filled with fidelities, love, nurturing, and times spent with one another, so also someone who has faith is faithful. Initial faith and discipleship, in other words, are two dimensions of the same response but not two distinct patches of cloth that must be sewn together "with pins and needles."

After Peter explains the event of the Holy Spirit at Pentecost, Luke tells us that the folks who heard Peter "were cut to the heart" and asked, "Brothers, what shall we do?" (Acts 2:37). Peter's words about the need to *repent* are famous (2:38 – 39):

Repent and be baptized, every one of you, in the name of Jesus Christ for the forgiveness of your sins. And you will receive the gift of the Holy Spirit. The promise is for you and your children and for all who are far off — for all whom the Lord our God will call.

In Acts 3:19 – 21, Peter says:

Repent, then, and turn to God, so that your sins may be wiped out, that times of refreshing may come from the Lord, and that he may send the Messiah, who has been appointed for you — even Jesus. Heaven must receive him until the time comes for God to restore everything, as he promised long ago through his holy prophets.

And in Acts 10:46b–48, while Peter is still preaching, the Holy Spirit comes down afresh on the audience, in some ways extending Pentecost to Gentiles, and Peter asks the *baptism* question:

> Then Peter said, "Surely no one can stand in the way of their being *baptized* with water. They have received the Holy Spirit just as we have." So he ordered that they *be baptized* in the name of Jesus Christ. Then they asked Peter to stay with them for a few days.

These three terms—believe, repent, baptize—are the terms the apostles used for *how* one entered into the gospel story. How are the three terms related? We are perhaps pushing against the grain of the Bible itself here, so I think we need to be cautious. It is not entirely clear to me that we can discern the relationship, but I will take a stab and put it this way: *faith* is the big idea with *repentance* and *baptism* as manifestations of that faith. The one who turns in *belief* to Christ *turns away from* (the word picture in the word *repent*) everything and everyone else—and Paul calls them to *turn away from* idols (Acts 14:15)—and the one who trusts in Christ obediently embodies that faith in *baptism*. To cut short what could be a long discussion, baptism embodies dying with Christ and being raised with Christ, as Romans 6 makes so abundantly clear.[73]

There is no substantive difference between what we've just summarized from Luke in the book of Acts and what the apostle Paul says about the proper response to God in the book of Romans (10:9–13):

> If you declare with your mouth, "Jesus is Lord," and believe in your heart that God raised him from the dead, you will be saved. For it is with your heart that you believe and are justified, and it is with your mouth that you profess your faith and are saved. As Scripture says, "Anyone who believes in him will never be put to shame." For there is no difference between Jew and Gentile—the same Lord is Lord of all and richly blesses all who call on him, for, "Everyone who calls on the name of the Lord will be saved."

But a first-century (Jewish) reader would have seen something in all of this that most of us would not see. In Acts 10–11 Peter *does not mention circumcision* when it comes to the proper response for Gentiles. Historians have been debating for a few decades just what

Jews required Gentile converts to do in order to convert to Judaism, but the one certain requirement for males was circumcision. Some of Peter's listeners would have taken strict notice that Peter permitted Gentile conversion into the Jesus community without requiring the kosher blade. That the issue of requiring Gentile converts to go under the knife emerges as a potentially community-dividing topic in Acts 15 does not surprise. That it does not emerge in Acts 10–11 does surprise. I tender a guess: Peter saw clear and unmistakable evidence of the gift of the Holy Spirit on these folks and said, "If repentance and baptism draw the Spirit down from the heavens, then we need nothing more."

THE APOSTLES PROMISE REDEMPTION IN A VARIETY OF TERMS

Those who hear the gospel and those who respond in faith, repentance, and baptism *are saved.* Neither our Plan of Salvation nor our Methods of Persuasion shaped the gospeling of Peter, but both the Plan of Salvation approach and Peter's gospeling offer the same benefits. And once again we are right back on top of 1 Corinthians 15: Peter promises the *forgiveness of sins* in Acts 2:38; 3:19; and 10:43. In addition, Peter promises his responders that they will be *filled with the Holy Spirit* (2:38–39; 10:44–47; 11:16–18) and will experience the ongoing *times of refreshing* (3:19). Paul says they will find *justification* (13:38–39).

In addition, in Acts 10:36 we read this as what Peter promises if they respond to the gospel Story of Jesus: "You know the message God sent to the people of Israel, announcing the good news of peace through Jesus Christ, who is Lord of all." Salvation means *peace.* It is fairly common for modern readers to think Peter is referring to the internal peace that comes to us as a result of making peace with God, and I don't doubt that Peter believed that happened. But that's not what this text is about. At Acts 10:36 "peace" refers to the peace of bringing Gentiles and Jews together, as found for instance in Ephesians 2:11–22. This Jewish-*and*-Gentile people of God, which both vexed Paul's relations with some Jerusalem-based believers and dominated his letters, including Romans, Colossians, and Ephesians, was anticipated in the Abrahamic blessing (Gen. 12:1–3), and yet it was never realized until the incorporation of Gentiles into the community of Jesus. That peace comes in the saving Story of Jesus.

There is so much more to be said about each of these terms, but our intent here is not an exhaustive study but a sketch. Furthermore, while those who do respond to the gospel are redeemed, rescued, saved, and justified, it is clear from Peter's and Paul's own sermons that the framing story is not so much salvation as the Story of Israel coming to completion in the Story of Jesus. That story, and that story alone, saves. Or better yet, Jesus saves, and it is the telling of his story that prompts people to respond in faith, repentance, and baptism and so be saved—forgiveness, the Spirit, refreshing, and the new community of God made of Jews and Gentiles alike.

CONCLUSION

This is the fourth leg for our chair: the apostolic gospel tradition, the gospel in the four Gospels, the gospel of Jesus, and now the gospeling sermons in the book of Acts. Each of these four witnesses tells us the same thing about the gospel. It is the Story of Israel that comes to completion in the saving Story of Jesus, who is Messiah of Israel, Lord over all, and the Davidic Savior. There is one and only one gospel, and it was preached by Jesus, by Paul, and by Peter. To gospel is to tell that story about Jesus. Salvation flows from that story, but that story is both bigger than and framed differently from the Plan-of-Salvation approach to the gospel. The apostles were the original evangelicals.

Most importantly, only by telling this apostolic gospel can we rebuild a gospel culture. This gospel culture does not displace salvation but puts salvation in the context of a gospel story that has a beginning (in creation and covenant with Israel), a middle (David), and a resolution (Jesus and final redemption).

How then we can we build a gospel culture? How can we construct a message and churches that are rooted in the apostolic gospel—the gospel that is Jesus, the gospel Jesus preached, and the gospel the apostles preached?

CHAPTER 9

GOSPELING
TODAY

THE TASK OF EVANGELISM, what I am calling "gospeling," is no less demanding and difficult today than it was in the time of Peter and Paul. It is also in no less need of creative adaptations to one's audience. Perhaps we need more of the boldness that came upon the apostles through a fresh blowing of the Spirit. Perhaps we need to pray as those early Christians prayed: "After they prayed, the place where they were meeting was shaken. And they were all filled with the Holy Spirit and spoke the word of God *boldly*" (Acts 4:31).

Or perhaps it is the almost complete absence of resurrection theology in much of gospeling today that explains our lack of boldness. At any rate, we need to recover more of that early, emboldened Christian resurrection gospel.

If we put this gospel now into one bundle, and if we focus on how that gospel was preached by the apostles, the book of Acts reveals that the gospel is, first of all, framed by *Israel's Story*: the narration of the saving Story of Jesus — his life, his death, his resurrection, his exaltation, and his coming again — as the completion of the Story of Israel.

Second, the gospel centers on the lordship of *Jesus*. In ways that anticipate the Nicene Creed, the gospel of Peter and Paul is anchored in an exalted view of Jesus. Jesus is seen as suffering, saving, ruling, and judging because he is the Messiah and the Lord and the Davidic Savior. He is now exalted at the right hand of God.

Third, gospeling involves *summoning people to respond*. Apostolic gospeling is incomplete until it lovingly but firmly summons those who hear the gospel to repentance, to faith in Jesus Christ, and to baptism.

Fourth, the gospel *saves and redeems*. The apostolic gospel promises forgiveness, the gift of God's Holy Spirit, and justification.

I rest my case now: these four points sketch the gospel wherever we look in the New Testament. This gospel is found in Paul's own words in 1 Corinthians 15, it is the gospel of the Gospels, it is the gospel of Jesus himself, it is the gospel of Peter, and it is the gospel of Paul—according to Luke's own sketch of Paul's sermons. There is one and only one gospel, and it was passed on from Jesus to the apostles to their churches. It is this gospel, and this gospel alone, that glues the New Testament into a unity.[74] If we want to be New Testament Christians, this gospel must once again become our gospel.

We are now prepared to compare our gospeling with their gospeling, and I will make six comparisons. We don't have to do everything as the apostles did, and neither do we have to abandon everything we are doing. But anyone who takes Scripture seriously needs to pause now and again to compare what he or she thinks with what the apostles taught, and when it comes to gospeling we have more than a little to learn. In fact, we need a grassroots commitment to transform our gospeling to get in line with the apostolic gospel.

COMPARISON 1: WHAT GOSPELING SEEKS TO ACCOMPLISH

There is a huge difference between the gospeling of Acts and our Plan of Salvation approach today, and alongside that difference, the gospel of Acts has almost no similarity to our Method of Persuasion. The difference can be narrowed to this single point: the gospeling of Acts, because it declares the saving significance of Jesus, Messiah and Lord, *summons listeners to confess Jesus as Messiah and Lord*, while our gospeling *seeks to persuade sinners to admit their sin and find Jesus as the Savior*.

We are not creating a false alternative here. The latter can be done within the former, but much of the soterian approach to evangelism today fastens on Jesus as (personal) Savior and dodges Jesus as Messiah and Lord. If there is any pervasive heresy today, it's right here. Anyone who can preach the gospel and not make Jesus' exalted lordship the focal point simply isn't preaching the apostolic gospel.

Within this general comparison I want to fix on two terms: the gospeling of the apostles in the book of Acts is bold *declaration* that leads to a summons while much of evangelism today is crafty *persuasion*. Once again, the latter can be done within the former, but the latter is too often done today without the former. The practical result is obvious: we need to do more telling about Jesus. We need to regain our confidence in the utter power of proclaiming that one Story of Jesus.

COMPARISON 2: WHAT FRAMES GOSPELING

Perhaps the most astounding observation is that the book of Acts reveals that *gospeling was not driven by the salvation story or the atonement story*. It was driven *by the Story of Israel*, and in fact makes most sense in that story. We soterian type of evangelicals need to awaken to the reality of how the Bible presents gospeling. In fact, the book of Acts has only hints of an atonement theology at work in the narration of the death of Jesus in gospeling (but cf. Acts 20:28).

While this absence might surprise us, and it might annoy you as a reader of this book, that absence stands proudly alongside the gospel summary of 1 Corinthians 15:3: "that Christ died for our sins according to Scripture." In Paul's own capsule summary of the gospel, we've got the death of Jesus, we've got Scripture's Story coming to completion, and we've got "for our sins" after the death of Jesus. That seems to be enough for the apostolic gospel tradition.

Look again at that gospel summary in 1 Corinthians 15: there is nothing direct about being reconciled to God or to others, nothing direct about being declared righteous, nothing about God's wrath being pacified, and nothing about being liberated from our entrapments to sin, self, the system, and Satan. To make these absences a little more obvious, there is also nothing in those sermons about God's love for us or God's grace, though grace appears often in the book of Acts as a summary of the gospel itself (cf. Acts 11:23; 13:43; 14:3, 26; 15:11; 20:24).

The book of Acts does not have an atonement theory shaping the fundamental gospeling events of Peter or Paul. Some will be offended by this—in fact, I have myself been offended at times by their approach, but I ask us all to reread the New Testament. These facts are in your Bible as much as they are in mine. I want to explain what is there and not use what is not there to explain what is there. I have written three books that touch on gospel themes: *Embracing Grace*, *A Community Called Atonement*, and a fat monograph on the historical Jesus called *Jesus and His Death*. In each of those books the gospeling in the book of Acts was given little more than a passing glance because I had not yet settled in my own mind how to frame the gospel in anything other than soterian and Jesus-as-Savior categories. So this book is a development of my own thinking, and it has shown me over and over that we need to relearn how to frame the gospel as the apostles did.

COMPARISON 3: GOSPELING, WRATH, AND JUDGMENT

Neither Peter nor Paul focuses on God's *wrath* when they evangelize in Acts, nor do they describe the saving Story of Jesus as an escape from hell. Having said that, and I have a nervous eye on the fire-and-brimstone form of the Method of Persuasion so common for certain kinds of evangelists, the great and final judgment is not far away from early Christian gospeling work. You can't avoid judgment in gospeling. Read Paul's sermon on the Areopagus one more time—in fact, I'll quote Acts 17:29–31 to make this clear:

> Therefore since we are God's offspring, we should not think that the divine being is like gold or silver or stone—an image made by human design and skill. In the past God overlooked such ignorance, but now he commands all people everywhere to repent. For he has set a day when he will judge the world with justice by the man he has appointed. He has given proof of this to everyone by raising him from the dead.

You can find this theme at times in the sermons of Acts—human beings must finally stand before God. Gospeling must involve the Story of final judgment in order for humans to see that they ultimately will stand before God and not before a human tribunal.

No one mastered, and at times overmastered and exploited, this approach to gospeling better than the Puritans and the revivalists. In fact, America's most famous preacher of hell is Jonathan Edwards, and his sermon "Sinners in the Hands of an Angry God" has made more people angry than have read the sermon.[75] I have before me a collection of his sermons, and my own reading of them has given me a completely different image of America's most famous sermon. His sermon "Heaven Is a World of Love" is breathtaking in beauty and scope and grace. In this collection I see a man in love with God, a man intoxicated with bringing glory to God, and a man whose religious affections were devoted to the good things of God.

Edwards's theology is not mine, and his imagery of God holding humans in the hands of providential fate and doing with them according to his arbitrary will is not easy to digest, but one cannot dismiss the presence of a final judgment in the gospeling of the apostles. Therefore, all extravagances aside, one cannot dismiss those who have been able to put before humans the reality of final judgment. Perhaps we need more of Edwards today, not less.

COMPARISON 4: THE PROBLEM GOSPELING RESOLVES

Another issue pertains to the *problem*. Just what the "problem" is that the apostles see resolved in the gospel is worthy of serious reconsideration when one studies the gospeling events of Acts. One can infer from the promises — forgiveness and the gift of the Holy Spirit and the times of refreshing — that the problems were sins and the absence of God's power and the need of new creation. We dare not minimize sins in gospeling; we dare not minimize our lack of God's gracious presence in the Spirit; we dare not minimize our deadness and need of new life in the new creation. But we would be mistaken to reduce these themes to nothing more than individualism. Peter's summary in Acts 5:29 – 32 sees forgiveness for "Israel." God is at work in his people and therefore in individuals, and we need to see that one of the problems is the people of God who need to become the true people of God. The New Testament expresses this new people of God in the word *church*.

But I would urge us to think much more deeply about the problem that the gospel resolved in light of our study so far. If the Story of Israel finds its completion in the Story of Jesus and if that is the gospel, we must find the problem within the fabric and contours of Israel's Story and not just in my needs in my story. We need to find the problem behind the solution Jesus offered. Jesus' word for the solution is *the kingdom*, or, if we frame as John did, *eternal life* (which, too, is more than personally living forever with God after we die). If kingdom is the solution, the problem was about the search for God's kingdom on earth and the problem was the absence of God's kingdom on earth. If eternal life is the solution, then the problem was death and the absence of God's abundant life and the worldliness of this world.

There is much more here to explore, and I want to dip into the discussion knowing that it would take a full book to work out some of this, and I will add more to this in the last chapter. What happens if we begin to rethink the "problem" in light of the fundamental solution? I will attempt to sketch an answer. Remember that *the fundamental solution in the gospel is that Jesus is Messiah and Lord*; this means there was a fundamental need for a ruler, a king, and a lord. The pressing need for the Jews of Jesus' day was for the Messiah-King and the Messiah-King's people in the Messiah-King's land. Now this might seem simplistic, but any reading of the Prophets, former or latter and major and minor, will show that the problem for the Story of Israel was a resolution to Israel's and Judah's problems.

The only way to answer this is to appeal to the story, and that story begins in Genesis 1–2. Recently Wheaton professor John Walton has pulled together in a readable format what scholars of the ancient world have known for a long time: the creation account of Genesis 1 depicts the world as a *cosmic temple*.[76] God places humans in his temple, but when he does he makes humans his *Eikons*, the God-bearers, and their responsibility is to relate to God, self, others, and the world *as co-rulers with God and as mediators of God's presence in God's cosmic temple.* Just in case you have forgotten the critical passage in this drama, I quote the whole thing from Genesis 1:26–30.

First, God forms humans into male and female as Eikons:

> Then God said, "Let us make mankind in our image, in our likeness, so that they may rule over the fish in the sea and the birds in the sky, over the livestock and all the wild animals, and over all the creatures that move along the ground."
>
> So God created mankind in his own image,
> in the image of God he created them;
> male and female he created them.

God then assigns Eikons a special task, and it is *the* fundamental human assignment:

> God blessed them and said to them, "Be fruitful and increase in number; fill the earth and subdue it. Rule over the fish in the sea and the birds in the sky and over every living creature that moves on the ground."
>
> Then God said, "I give you every seed-bearing plant on the face of the whole earth and every tree that has fruit with seed in it. They will be yours for food. And to all the beasts of the earth and all the birds in the sky and all the creatures that move along the ground — everything that has the breath of life in it — I give every green plant for food." And it was so.

The so-called fall of Genesis 3 is not just an act of sinning against God's command, a moral lapse, but a betrayal of our fundamental **kingly** and priestly roles. Instead of mediating God to the serpent, instead of taking our assignment of ruling God's good garden on God's behalf, Adam and Eve tried to elevate themselves to God's role. The issue is not just that we were sinners; we were *usurpers* in the garden.

But God forgives by banning us from the opportunity to live forever as cracked Eikons, as broken image-bearers. So he sends us east of Eden into the world *with the same task*. But over and over again we humans fail to rule properly and fail to mediate properly, and over and over again we become usurpers. The moment we usurp, we deconstruct the world God has created. So God chooses — and here I will leave the mystery to God — Abraham in order to form a nation of "kings and priests." That is, the assignment God gave to Adam was transferred to Abraham and to Israel.

Then God gives Moses the important task of leading a rescue, of giving the Torah to Israel, and of helping them find their way to the Promised Land. But it's all the same task: in the heart of Exodus we find this assignment all over again: to be kings and priests—as a people:

> "You yourselves have seen what I did to Egypt, and how I carried you on eagles' wings and brought you to myself. Now if you obey me fully and keep my covenant, then out of all nations you will be my treasured possession. Although the whole earth is mine, you will be for me a *kingdom of priests* and a holy nation." These are the words you are to speak to the Israelites. (Ex. 19:4–6)

But like Adam and Eve and like the folks who mucked things up in Genesis 4–11, so also Israel fails to be the priestly kingdom. So God charts a different path and narrows it down to the Samuel-Saul, rather unwillingly it appears (because God alone is to be king), but then even more importantly to David. David does just OK and then Solomon ... it gets messy real fast. This kingly and priestly Story of Israel is one long set of maybes and almosts and you-did-well, but in the end Israel's failure leads to God's sending the one true representative Israelite, Jesus.

It is precisely here that Jesus' being Messiah makes its only storied sense, and it is also precisely here that the gospel finally makes sense. Not only is Jesus Messiah, but Jesus over and over in the New Testament is the one true Eikon of God. What the apostles were telling us is that the assignment God gave Adam, the assignment transferred to Abraham, Israel, and Moses, and then to David has now been transferred to and perfectly fulfilled by Jesus. I will quote three texts, each of which is a profound gospel text, a text that gospels a gospel about Jesus Christ as Eikon and as Messiah and Lord over all. I begin with Philippians 2:6–11, where the whole Story of Israel is told into the Story of Jesus as the Eikon of God, who is Lord over all:

> Who, being in very nature God,
>> did not consider equality with God something to be
>>> used to his own advantage;
>> rather, he made himself nothing
>>> by taking the very nature of a servant,

being made in human likeness.
And being found in *appearance as a man*,
   he humbled himself
   by becoming obedient to death —
      even death on a cross!
Therefore God exalted him to the highest place
   and gave him the name that is above every name,
that at the name of Jesus every knee should bow,
   in heaven and on earth and under the earth,
and every tongue acknowledge that *Jesus Christ is Lord*,
   to the glory of God the Father.

Also Colossians 1:15–20, where again we find Jesus as Eikon and Jesus as Lord over all:

The Son is the *image* of the invisible God, the firstborn *over* all creation. For in him all things were created: things in heaven and on earth, visible and invisible, whether thrones or powers or rulers or authorities; *all things have been created through him and for him*. He is *before* all things, and in him *all things hold together*. And he is the *head of the body, the church*; he is the beginning and the firstborn from among the dead, so that in everything he might have the supremacy. For God was pleased to have *all his fullness dwell in him*, and through him to reconcile to himself all things, whether things on earth or things in heaven, by making peace through his blood, shed on the cross.

And then also 2 Corinthians 3:18–4:6, where Jesus as God's image is also a display of God's glory and the Spirit works in us to transform us into the Eikonic image of Jesus Christ, who is Lord:

And we all, who with unveiled faces contemplate *the Lord's glory*, are being transformed into his *image with ever-increasing glory*, which comes from the Lord, who is the Spirit.

Therefore, since through God's mercy we have this ministry, we do not lose heart. Rather, we have renounced secret and shameful ways; we do not use deception, nor do we distort the word of God. On the contrary, by setting forth the truth plainly we commend ourselves to everyone's conscience in the sight of God. And even if our gospel is veiled, it is veiled to those who are perishing. The god of this age has blinded the minds of unbelievers, so that they cannot see the light of the gospel that displays the glory of Christ, who is the *image of God*. For what we preach is not ourselves, but *Jesus Christ as Lord*, and ourselves as your servants for Jesus' sake. For God, who said, "Let light shine out of darkness," made his light shine in our hearts to give us the light of the knowledge of *God's glory displayed in the face of Christ*.

Do you see how frequently these preeminent gospeling texts usher us into the glories of seeing the exalted status of Jesus as Messiah and Lord? It's obvious from these texts that the Story is about King Jesus, about God sending his Son to "become" King Jesus.

I have but one more point to make here, and it takes the messianic and kingly assignment that Jesus alone accomplished perfectly and *amazingly assigns it back to us — the people of God*, this time seen in Revelation 5:9–10 and 20:6:

And they sang a new song, saying:
   "You are worthy to take the scroll
      and to open its seals,
   because you were slain,
      and with your blood you purchased for God
      persons from every tribe and language and people
         and nation.
   You have made them to be a kingdom and priests to serve our God,
   and they will reign on the earth."

Blessed and holy are those who share in the first resurrection. The second death has no power over them, *but they will be priests of God and of Christ and will reign with him for a thousand years.*

The messianic, lordly, and kingly confession of Jesus is not incidental to the Bible. It is the point of the Bible, and the gospel is the good news that Jesus is that Messiah, that Lord, and that King. We are his subjects. The question over and over in the Bible is: "Who is the rightful Lord of this cosmic temple?" The answer shifts in the pages of Israel's Story until it comes to Jesus, and we get not a full stop but an exclamation point: Jesus is the Messiah and Lord!

Yes, the problem is our sin; yes, we need to be forgiven of sinfulness and our sins. But that sin and that forgiveness are connected to our lordly assignments and to our priestly responsibilities and to our flailing and failing attempts to usurp God's tasks to make them ours. The only one worthy to sit on that throne is King Jesus.

My summary point of comparison: gospeling declares that Jesus is that rightful Lord, gospeling summons people to turn from their idols to worship and live under that Lord who saves, and gospeling actually puts us in the co-mediating and co-ruling tasks under our Lord Jesus. When we reduce the gospel to only personal salvation, as soterians are tempted to do, we tear the fabric out of the Story of the Bible and we cease even needing the Bible. I don't know of any other way to put it.

COMPARISON 5: GOSPEL AND EMPIRE

Here's a point that flows directly from the previous one. There is much to-do today about the anti-imperial slant of the apostolic gospel and earliest Christianity. This theme can be found among some of the most recognizable scholars, like Tom Wright and Richard Horsley, as well as in some of the most recognizable preachers, like Rob Bell in his Nooma video "You." A common element to this approach is that what the apostles were really claiming, if you pick up the clues and the hints and read between the lines and know the historical contexts, was that if Jesus was Lord, then Caesar was not! Some of these claims about Jesus, some scholars are arguing today, consciously and clearly were aimed at the claims by Romans that Caesar was divine and worthy of worship. In other words, the first Christians wanted to subvert the empire with an alternative politics.

What are we to make of this? Let's keep in mind that no one would ever deny that *an* implication of the gospel declaration that Jesus is Lord is that Caesar is not. The issue here is how *conscious, overt, and intentional* this anti-imperial theme is to the gospeling of the first Christians.

This approach has something important to tell us about what it means to declare Jesus as Lord. But there must be some cautionary red flags waved before we can come to terms with how overt this anti-imperial theme is. First, it is hard for me to think that Paul had a sharp anti-imperial edge to his gospel if he was able to tell the

Romans, of all the churches to whom he wrote (!), that they were to submit to the emperor and that the one who rebels against the emperor is rebelling against God (see Rom. 13:1–7). Furthermore, there simply isn't any overt criticism of the emperor cult in either Peter or Paul in their sermons in Acts.

Nonetheless, one might argue that the blame both Peter and Paul lay on the temple establishment for killing Jesus is anti-imperialism. In addition, Paul's anti-idolatry language in Acts 14:15–17 "may" be aimed at the emperor cult, and his address at the Areopagus, bringing up idols, does support the anti-imperial application of the gospel to the Romans, who were worshiping the idols. Caesar and the Messiah, one on a throne in Rome and the other on a cross in Jerusalem. Yes, they confront one another. Yes, the implication that Jesus is Lord cuts into the heart of the Roman imperial cult.

G. N. Stanton has traced a possible anti-imperial social context in the very word that animates this book, the word *gospel*. When the Christians began to use *gospel* publicly, he concludes, they did so at almost the same time something highly significant was happening in the Jewish and Roman worlds. I quote Stanton's elegant summary:[77]

> When Christian Greek-speaking Jews in Jerusalem and/or Antioch were probably first starting to use the noun "gospel" in the singular to refer both to the act of proclamation of God's glad tiding concerning Jesus Christ and to its content, Gaius ordered his statue to be erected in the temple in Jerusalem. He was considered by many of his subjects to be a "saviour and benefactor." His accession had been hailed as "good news," and as marking the dawn of a new era, but his antics undermined that acclamation. So, from a very early point indeed, Christian use of the gospel word group may have formed part of a counter-story to the story associated with the imperial cult.

Yes, Stanton's sketch is plausible. Yes, the lordship of Jesus cuts into every idol and everything that would become God, including worship of the Roman emperor. And yes, when Peter's gospeling in Acts 10 brings in words for Jesus like "peace" and "Lord of all" and "doing good," which translates the word *benefactor*, we have to wonder if the chosen words are subtle jabs at emperor worship. One could say Peter was (indirectly and quietly) claiming that all these things came to us through Jesus and not through Caesar. I agree with how Michael Bird puts this: "Nero did not throw Christians to the lions because they confessed that 'Jesus is Lord of my heart.' It was rather because they confessed that 'Jesus is Lord of all,' meaning that Jesus was Lord even over the realm Caesar claimed as his domain of absolute authority."[78]

But some of these scholars see something far more consciously subversive about the Christian gospel of Jesus and the apostles. No matter how much I'm personally inclined to want this set of ideas to be true, I'm not convinced the anti-imperial theme was as conscious to the apostles as some are suggesting. I would prefer to see the apostles just come out and say it. It's not like Peter and Paul were afraid of anyone, let alone of some pagan ruler like Caesar. Luke tells us to the end of his story in Acts that the apostle Paul just kept on preaching that Jesus was Lord and that he was the Lord of the kingdom of God.[79] To proclaim the gospel entails that Caesar — in whatever guise such an autocrat presents himself — is not. But to claim the gospel was intentionally subversive stretches the evidence.

COMPARISON 6: TALK ABOUT JESUS

Our sixth and final comparison is this: the apostles evangelized by telling the Story of Jesus. Our gospel preaching and evangelism tend to tell the story of how to be saved personally. There is a major difference between the Story of Jesus and a Plan of Salvation, and it is a difference that deserves more space than we can possibly give it here.

First, our gospeling tends to reduce and aim at one and only one target: the sinner's heart. Evangelism's focus is on the individual person, and it is on getting that person to admit that he or she is a sinner and then to receive Jesus Christ as Savior and solution to the sin problem. In the words of Dallas Willard, our gospel is about sin management.[80] But the apostolic gospel can't be reduced to a gospel of sin management because it was a gospel of Jesus-declaration (that included the defeat of sin and death).

Don't get me wrong, the apostolic gospel did promise the forgiveness of sins. But it did so by telling a (saving) story about Jesus. I am always struck by Luke's recounting of how the Jerusalemites responded to Peter's first gospel sermon in Acts 2:37: "When the people heard this [gospel about the Story of Israel coming to completion in the Story of Jesus], they were *cut to the heart* and said to Peter and the other apostles, 'Brothers, what shall we do?'" An implication is obvious: telling the Story of Jesus is anointed by God to awaken sin in the person who hears the Story of Jesus. Instead of focusing on their sin, though Peter does lay blame on them for crucifying Jesus or implicates them in that dreadful deed, Peter focuses on Jesus, and the Jesus Story awakens a consciousness of sin and a need for Jesus to be their Messiah, Lord, and Savior.

Second, the question that many are asking today reveals that there's not enough Jesus in our gospel. The question is this: Did Jesus preach the gospel? If we are tempted for even a passing moment to wonder if the Gospels preach the gospel, then we have fallen from the apostolic gospel. Why? It was the apostolic generation that called Mark (and probably Matthew) the "gospel." Why? Because the gospel is the completion of Israel's Story in the Story of Jesus, and that is precisely what the Gospels in fact do. But if we are asking that question, it is probably because we have succumbed to the Plan of Salvation gospel, in a reduced soterian form, as the one and only gospel.

We need to talk more about Jesus and know that telling others about Jesus is half the battle when it comes to fear of evangelism. We can improve our evangelism simply by learning to approach the gospel in the apostolic manner. That's the easy part. The hard part is creating a gospel culture that expands (and supplants) our reduced salvation culture. I have a few suggestions in the last chapter.

CHAPTER 10

CREATING A GOSPEL CULTURE

IT WAS RAINING.

It was Ireland.

It was expected and it didn't matter. It was Monday morning and my wife, Kris, and I were in the car with our friend Patrick Mitchel, and we were headed north from Dublin to a place called Newgrange. I was so tied up with preparation for lectures and talks and sermons for Ireland that I really didn't even know what we were going to see at Newgrange. Kris did because she takes care of such things for our family. She told me earlier that morning that we would be seeing "some kind of burial site." Did I mention that the rain was appropriate?

About five thousand years ago, close to the famous River Boyne and not all that far from the eastern coast of Ireland, a group of people built a passageway into a man-made hill that appeared to be a burial tomb, and we were on our way to see it. We met up at the center with three others: Andy and Louise Halpin and Linda Basdeo. We were escorted by bus over to the tomb, where we were given a masterful tour. The tour was supplemented by the expertise of Andy, an archaeologist. Roughly the size of about half of a football field, the tomb was originally a cone-shaped burial ground.

Two facts about Newgrange's tomb stood out for me: first was the ingenuity of those who built this tomb. We entered through a narrow and low passageway, but above us was another "passageway." That upper passageway, we were about to learn, was for the sun alone. Incredibly, on one day every year (unless it was raining!), at the time of the winter solstice, the sun passes through that upper passageway into the heart of the tomb and tosses its morning light on the precise place of burial. (Remember, this is five thousand years ago, so the knowledge, skill, and the manpower to build this passage tomb remains a marvel.)

But what struck me most was this: no one really knows what this passage tomb means. There are no records of the area being inhabited at that time, and there is no written record about what anything meant. Which means this: there are two passageways into an inner vault, and there are some curious triskele-like carvings, or three interlocking spirals, on huge stones at various locations. That's all we've got. We've got no interpretations of anything. Some think the spirals are abstract art while others think they are symbolic of something more significant. But as we wandered around the site with Andy, our archaeologist friend, we were often struck by his responses. When I asked a few times about something we had seen, his response was the same: "We just don't know. There are theories but no one knows for sure."

Here's my point: we have a formidable accomplishment by humans some five thousand years ago, but *no one knows what it means because there is no written record to interpret their remarkable construction.*

When we were done at Newgrange, we had lunch. It was still raining; it was Ireland, and it was expected. Our next stop was a few miles away at a monastery called Monasterboice, a late-fifth-century monastery. It is home to two of Ireland's "high crosses," one of which is Ireland's finest high cross, the eighteen-foot-high Muire-dach's Cross, dating probably to about AD 900. Not only is this cross noted for the Celtic ring that props up the horizontal beams of the stone cross, but every inch of the cross has more artwork. The very top of the cross is actually a replica of a church building, while the rest of the cross contains artistic renditions of central events in the Story of the Bible. In the middle of the cross itself is a scene of the last judgment of Christ—those to the right go to heaven and those to the left to hell. There are a number of scenes, including the sin of Adam and Eve and Moses striking the rock.

Now to our point: we have a cross, which by itself, like Newgrange, would mean nothing more than a symbol of capital punishment. It would be hard to know what a cross might mean. But because all over the cross are scenes from the Bible and because the Story of the Bible comes to completion in the Story of Jesus on this cross, we *know what this archaeological artifact means.* Nietzsche may be right that sometimes our interpretations bury the text, but *without interpretation this "cross text" means nothing.* This cross (a text), unlike Newgrange's passage tomb (another text), is interpreted so we can know what it means.

This leads me to the point these two points were designed to lead to: *the gospel is Jesus' and the apostles' interpretation of the story of life.* The gospel is the secret to life, and the gospel is the way to the truth and the life. We must know this gospel if we are to build a gospel culture. So to those two ideas—the gospel and a gospel culture—I now turn to conclude this book.

THE GOSPEL SKETCHED

It's time now to put this entire gospel together in a way more completely than I did in the previous chapter. There is no way to reduce this to four points, and there is also no way to sketch the gospel in a minute or two. To grasp the gospel we have to grasp what God is doing in this world, and that means we've got a story to tell.

I have heard the story told about Robert Webber, one of Wheaton College's most influential (and provocative) professors in the last half century, that he was in his basement one day when someone asked him to explain the Gospel. He asked the person, "Do you have an hour?" So he took about an hour with this person to explain the great good news from creation to consummation.[81] I won't take an hour here, but I tell this story to emphasize that the assumption on the part of many that the gospel can be reduced to a note card—or a napkin—is already off on the wrong track. Here goes:

In the beginning God. In the beginning God created everything we see and some things we can't yet see. In the beginning God turned what existed into a cosmic temple. In the beginning God made two Eikons, Adam and Eve. In the beginning God gave Adam and Eve one simple task: to govern this world on God's behalf.

But Adam and Eve thought better and usurped God's prerogative. They usurped the rule of God in this world and, instead of listening to the good word of God, they listened to the serpent and to themselves and ruined their opportunity to govern as God's co-governors in Eden. For one dark moment the Eikons acted the part of God. So God banished them from Eden and cast them into the world as we now know it. God would find another way for his Eikons to co-govern the world.

Sadly, all the descendants of Adam and Even have proven their pattern. We are all usurpers. We all want to rule, not under God as God's under-governors but as gods and goddesses. Still, God gave Adam and Eve's descendants the opportunity to right the ship, but they cascaded into a nightmare of usurpations that all but ruined their opportunity to govern on God's behalf. But God is gracious. Just as he gave Adam and Eve a new opportunity after their usurpation in Eden, so God gave all the descendants more opportunities. Usurpation was the name of the descendants' game, and with their building of the Tower of Babel, which took Adam and Eve's usurpation to a new level, God chose another way of establishing his rule on earth. How?

God chose Abraham. Then God chose Israel. God would give Israel the task of governing. So God created a covenant between himself and Abraham and Israel, a covenant that was to be eternal and redemptive. God promised to be with Israel as the One who was for Israel. What God did was to transfer the governing assignment given to Adam and Eve to Abraham and Israel. As the original Eikons were to govern this world on God's behalf, so Abraham and Israel were to bless the nations. They did this well at times, and at other times they acted like usurpers and chose to do things their own way.

As God's chosen people, God was with them when they were slaves in Egypt and God was for them, so he liberated them from

Egypt through the hand of Moses. God wanted them to live properly as a kingdom of priests, so he gave them the Torah and renewed the covenant with Israel at Mount Sinai. This Torah was to govern them in the land of Israel and, if they allowed it to govern them, they would flourish and would be able to bless the nations. But they did not do well because they didn't let the good Torah of God govern them. This second arrangement wasn't working either.

When Israel asked for a king like other nations, God at first balked, but eventually gave what the usurpers wanted: a human king. In his own mysterious grace, though, God chose to use this kingly wish and made one of their kings, David, the sort of king God wanted for them. This was the third form of governing on God's behalf. But David was a descendant of Adam and Eve, so he too became a usurper and messed up the kingly reign. He passed the throne on to someone who messed up even more, Solomon. One king after another, some of them good and some of them bad, governed God's people Israel and Judah. But each of them proved to be a usurper too, so God sent prophets to them to warn them that there was only one governor, one true King, one and only one God—and his name was YHWH.

Sometimes God had to discipline Israel to get the people's attention. Sometimes his discipline worked, like the exile in Babylon. It led to nothing less than a spiritual revival among those who returned to the land, but that revival wore off too because they were all usurpers. Perhaps they knew they were to govern not only the Promised Land but also the world, but they struggled so much to govern the land they never even entertained—except in brief poetic moments in prophets like Isaiah—governing the world on God's behalf. Within a few centuries Israel had seemingly forgotten the assignment God had given to Adam and Eve, the assignment that they were a priestly kingdom designed to bless the world.

After years of deafening silence, God moved into the final plan and suddenly broke into history with someone who was both descendant and non-descendant, someone who would rule rightly and not as a usurper. God sent to Israel Jesus, through Mary and Joseph, and God told Mary through an angel that her son, Jesus, would someday rule on God's behalf as Messiah.

But even though Jesus did exactly what God had told him to do, neither Israel nor the Gentiles around Israel accepted him as Messiah. (This theme consistently reveals that we are all usurpers and we don't want someone telling us what's best for us. We seem to be incurable usurpers.) Though Jesus was a man known to do good everywhere he went, and though he healed and rescued people from all sorts of problems, and though he brought people to the table who were forgiven and saved and healed and made new again and turned from usurpers to lovers, the descendants—both Roman and Jewish—decided they'd be better off putting him to death. They feared he'd deconstruct their usurpations, so they killed him in the most despicable of manners by crucifying him naked on a cross outside Jerusalem on Golgotha. The usurpers were in control and the descendants had descended to their lowest.

What the usurpers and descendants didn't know was that Jesus was actually entering into their usurpations and the death they deserved for their sins. He was dying their death, he was shouldering their sins and the punishment due their sins, and he was absorbing the just wrath of God against all sin. What they didn't know was that God could reverse their usurpations and reverse their death and start all over again. What they didn't know was that this way of dying as a servant was to become the only true way of living and making peace in this world. What they didn't know was that the cross was the crown and that power comes only when it is surrendered. They didn't know this. No one did. Not even Jesus' closest followers. What the usurpers didn't know was that they had met their match in King Jesus, who was about to usher in an alternative kingdom.

To start the world all over again, God, the God who graciously gave Adam and Eve another chance and the God who rescued Israel from the clutches of Egypt and the God who whistled for Israelites to return from Babylon, that same God—YHWH, the Father of Jesus Christ—erupted the normal categories of history one more time. He raised Jesus back to life to end the dominion of death, to prove that the usurpers would not have the last word, and to show that the descendants could have a whole new (creation) lineage. To make this altogether clear, Jesus appeared to hosts of the descendants and then he was taken up into the presence of God.

What this story shows is that what usurpers fear the most is the godness of God but, paradoxically, what usurpers most want is the godness of God, and Jesus was that God, and that is why Jesus as Messiah and Lord is the gospel. We finally had the King this earth needed. He was exalted to reign over the world, over both Jews as Messiah and over Gentiles as Lord. And he summoned all people to accept his forgiving, kindly, peaceful, gracious, transforming rule. If people would but turn to him, they would be forgiven and their usurpations would be forgotten forever. To create this new society, the kingdom society, the church society, Jesus sent to his people the Holy Spirit to empower them and transform them from usurpers into servants of God's love, peace, justice, and holiness. This was the alternative politics and the right way to govern the world on God's behalf: by loving others with everything we've got.

And this same God chose to do things all over again with his new creation people: he chose to give them a second chance, which is one way of talking about the magnificent theme of God's grace. He chose to let them be people of the kingdom, called the church, and he summoned them to believe in Jesus, to turn from their usurpations, and to so identify with Jesus that they would enter into his death and into his resurrection and through that find new life. Most importantly, though Jesus was the true king, the true Messiah, the true Eikon, and the true Lord, God gave to Jesus' people the assignment he had given to Adam and Eve. They were Eikons like Adam and Eve but with a major difference: they had the Holy Spirit. This Holy Spirit could transform them into the visible likeness of Jesus himself. As Christlike Eikons they are assigned to rule on God's behalf in this world. They do this by listening to this story, by living out this story as their story, and by spreading the good news of this story.

They now rule in an imperfect world in an imperfect way as imperfect Eikons. But someday the perfect Eikon will come back, and he will rescue his Eikons and set them up one more time in this world. This time, though, it will be right because Jesus will be the temple, and the garden will become the eternal city, and it will be filled with peace, love, joy, and holiness. All usurpations will end, and everyone will serve Jesus in the power of the Spirit to the glory of God the Father. Humans will govern on God's behalf in the way of Jesus.

Forever.

A GOSPEL CULTURE

That's the gospel.

A gospel culture emerges from that culture in the following ways.

PEOPLE OF THE STORY

First, *we have to become People of the Story*. One of the most common responses I've had to lecturing about the gospel occurs when someone approaches me to say something like this: "Scot, thanks for your lecture. During that lecture I committed myself to reading the Bible from front to back for the first time." To become a gospel culture we've got to begin with becoming people of the Book, but not just as a Book but as the story that shapes us. Sean Gladding's new book, *The Story of God, The Story of Us*, might be your needed push-off because he sketches the Bible's Story and then explains what happens in his subtitle: *Getting Lost and Found in the Bible*.[82] Exactly, and that's what we are talking about: the gospel is all about the Story of Israel coming to its resolution in the Story of Jesus and our letting that story become our story. To come to terms with this story-shaped gospel, we will have to become People of the Story.

PEOPLE OF THE STORY OF JESUS

Second, *we need to immerse ourselves even more into the Story of Jesus*. The gospel is that the Story of Israel comes to its definitive completeness in the Story of Jesus, and this means we have to become People of the Story-that-is-complete-in-Jesus. There is one and only one way to become People of the Story of Jesus: we need to soak ourselves in the Story of Jesus by reading, pondering, digesting, and mulling over in our heads and hearts the Four Gospels. Genuine soaking in this story always leads to the Story of Israel because it is only in that story that the Story of Jesus makes sense.

A brief example. The temptation story of Jesus is found in Matthew 4:1–11 and Luke 4:1–13, with a brief glimpse into it at Mark 1:12–13. All my life I've heard folks suggest that Jesus underwent those temptations to teach us how to endure temptations ourselves. Fine, that might be true, but it has nothing—so far as I can see—to do with the text itself. We need to become People of the Story before we can become people of the Story of Jesus. People of the story make two connections when they hear (or read) about Jesus' temptations. The weaker connection is with the experience of Adam and Eve in the garden of Eden. The presence of the serpent and Satan in these two texts makes for a connection.

But there is a much stronger connection, and it is this connection that makes this story come alive for People of the Story. Jesus three times in this temptation narrative quotes and draws from the experience of Israel in the wilderness. Jesus quotes Deuteronomy 8:3, then Deuteronomy 6:16 and 6:13. These are the "clues" to understand what Jesus is experiencing, and what he's experiencing is a second wilderness experience. The temptation story of Jesus reveals Jesus to be the Second Israel who goes through the forty-day test as Israel went through the forty-year test, but with one glaring, gospel difference: Jesus is obedient while Israel usurped time and time again. Much more could be said but need not: what I'm illustrating is that People of the Story see the Story of Jesus as the story that completes Israel's Story.

I see another way for us to become people of the Story of Jesus. For some of my readers this will be a bit annoying, but I want to ask you to rethink your instinctive reaction. We need to see the wisdom of the church's decision to follow a church calendar. My home church had two "church calendar" events: prophecy conference in the fall and missionary/revival conference in the spring. Of course, I'm kidding. Well, only partly. We did only "keep" two events: Christmas and Easter. I don't recall a Good Friday service at church when I was growing up, and I had never even heard of Maundy Thursday until I was in England during college and I got to preach at a church called Maundy Baptist. It had six or so people, but they didn't want to risk my bad sermon on a big church. Anyway, the church calendar, if examined briefly, is entirely structured around the Story of Jesus. That is, the *church calendar is a gospeling event too.*[83]

The church calendar is all about the Story of Jesus, and I know of nothing—other than regular soaking in the Bible—that can "gospelize" our life more than the church calendar. It begins with Advent, then Christmas, then Epiphany, then After Epiphany, then Lent, then the Great Triduum (Maundy Thursday, Good Friday, and the Paschal Vigil on Saturday evening), Easter, and then After Pentecost—with Ordinary Time shaping the calendar until Advent. Ordinary Time is the time to focus on the life and teachings of Jesus. Anyone who is half aware of the calendar in a church that is consciously devoted to focusing on these events in their theological and biblical contexts will be exposed every year to the whole gospel, to the whole Story of Israel coming to its saving completion in the Story of Jesus.

I wrote *One.Life* to help us become more attuned to the Story of Jesus.[84] If we become a gospel culture, we will become more attuned to the Story of Jesus and to how he "defines" what it means to be a Christian. Here is how I defined it: a Christian is one who follows Jesus by devoting his or her One.Life:

- to the kingdom of God, fired by Jesus' own imagination,
- to a life of loving God and loving others,
- to a society shaped by justice, especially for those who have been marginalized,
- to peace, and
- to a life devoted to acquiring wisdom in the context of a local church.

This life can only by discovered by being empowered by God's Spirit.

The next three suggestions deal with how we can develop a gospel culture by becoming people of the Story of Jesus.

PEOPLE OF THE CHURCH'S STORY

Third, *we need to see how the apostles' writings take the Story of Israel and the Story of Jesus into the next generation and into a different culture, and how this generation led all the way to our generation.* There is a powerful undercurrent today that is unsettling many of us: that undercurrent is a "Jesus only" approach to the Bible. The gospel is that the Story of Israel comes to completion in the Story of Jesus, but that gospel is not only the Story of Jesus. What is more: Jesus clearly told his disciples, and I think here of John 14–17; Matthew 28:16–20; and Acts 1:8, that *his story was to continue in the story of the church.*

We have a responsibility to Jesus to let the Story-of-Jesus-that-goes-on-and-on in the Church shape our Story. Yes, the church's story must be freshly checked against the gospel story of Jesus, but we have no right to ignore what God has been doing in the community of Jesus since the day he sent the Spirit to empower it, ennoble it, and guide it. This begins with fresh commitments to read the apostolic writings in the New Testament, and that means from Acts to Revelation.

A proper reading of these books means we see them as *continuations and fresh applications of the Story of Jesus in new contexts.* Gabe Lyons has a new book called *The Next Christians,*[85] and Gabe's expression "next Christians" is a good one for us in learning how to read what God has done: the good news is that *God has always raised up a generation of next Christians* who have been God's faithful witnesses to the gospel Story of Jesus for their generation. How can we come to terms with this history of the church, this people whose story leads to our story? I recommend you purchase a copy of a standard church history text, like Justo Gonzalez's highly recommended *The Story of Christianity*[86] or Chris Armstrong's representative volume on "patron saints,"[87] but I would urge you to make a lifetime commitment and not just a one-time commitment. Make a decision to know our story from Adam to the newest baptized Christian in your church. We need more of us to be curious about our ancestors. This will help us build a gospel culture.

We need also to know our creeds. As I said earlier, many of us are nervous about creeds, but the wisdom of the church is on the side of the value of creeds and confessions of the faith. So I would urge you to get online, google the Apostles' Creed or the Nicene Creed, and read them. Memorize one of them if you can. Then read other creeds like the great Reformation Confessions or even more recent confessions like *The Lausanne Covenant* or the *Manilla Manifesto.* You may not like the idea of a creed or you may not like the public recitation of a creed, and you may well have the experience many of us have had of standing in a church reciting a creed aloud when you know full well that some who are standing there reciting it don't believe half of it. But you do have a responsibility—if you want to be part of creating a gospel culture—to know what the gospel has done to the church throughout the ages.

DEVELOPING COUNTER STORIES

Fourth, *we need to counter the stories that bracket our story and that reframe our story.* Our culture offers us a myriad of false stories rooted in superficial worldviews. These stories, more often than not, refuse entrance to the gospel story or reshape that gospel story or seek overtly to destroy that story. But a gospel culture can resist those stories by announcing the gospel story as the true story. Or, in the words of the apostle Paul:

> The weapons we fight with are not the weapons of the world. On the contrary, they have divine power to demolish strongholds. We demolish arguments and every pretension that sets itself up against the knowledge of God, and *we take captive every thought to make it obedient to Christ.* (2 Cor. 10:4–5)

What are those stories?

- Individualism—the story that "I" am the center of the universe
- Consumerism—the story that I am what I own
- Nationalism—the story that my nation is God's nation
- Moral relativism—the story that we can't know what is universally good
- Scientific naturalism—the story that all that matters is matter
- New Age—the story that we are gods
- Postmodern tribalism—the story that all that matters is what my small group thinks
- Salvation by therapy—the story that I can come to my full human potential through inner exploration

I have taken these "hidden worldviews" from Steve Wilkens' and Mark Sanford's book, *Hidden Worldviews.*[88] But I'm less concerned with getting them all on paper than I am with recognizing that these worldviews need to be countered with the gospel story. How can we do this? That is, after the above three considerations, there are a few more things we can do to build a gospel culture.

The first thing is to emphasize *baptism*. What I mean here is Romans 6 as the articulation of Matthew 28:16–20. Jesus told his disciples to baptize disciples, but it was Paul who explained how *baptism was a gospeling act*. How so? Paul saw baptism as being baptized into the death of Jesus and emerging from the waters as being co-raised with Jesus Christ. This act of baptism isn't just about personal confession and personal faith. The public act of baptism is *in and of itself a public declaration of the saving Story of Jesus*. If done right, baptism gospels the gospel in a public manner.

Alongside baptism, I would emphasize the *Eucharist*. To be sure, there's even more debate about Eucharist than baptism, but let's get to the bottom of Eucharist for one moment. Jesus tells us that Eucharist, his Last Supper, was about ingesting his blood and his body, and in doing so it was participation in the saving and liberating significance of his story as completing Israel's (Passover) Story. Then the apostle Paul tells us something we perhaps ignore at our own peril: "For whenever you eat this bread and drink this cup, you proclaim the Lord's death until he comes" (1 Cor. 11:26).

Amazingly, Paul tells the Corinthians, the same ones who were about to hear about the gospel a few chapters later, that *ingesting the bread and wine was itself gospeling*. Whenever we partake in Eucharist, we are gospeling the death of the Lord Jesus Christ.

We can build a gospel culture if we emphasize baptism and Eucharist as the counter stories to the cultural stories that flood the Internet and media every day. In those acts we embody the Story of Israel coming to completion in the saving Story of Jesus.

Embrace the Story

Finally, *we need to embrace this story so that we are saved and can be transformed by the gospel story*. This book is not an exercise in theological speculation to determine who is right and who is wrong. Instead, this book is a plea that we will both discern the apostolic gospel and embrace that gospel so deeply we are wholly transformed into the image of Christ himself. A gospel culture can only be created if we are thoroughly converted ourselves.

Jesus, Peter, and Paul. They have been the focus of our attention. If we buy into their gospel vision, we are summoned by each to believe, to repent, and to be baptized into the name of the Father, the Son, and the Spirit. To be saved we must respond in faith. Saying it like this looks at the gospel and our response from the angle of what we are called to do, but there's another side: our response is prompted and attended by the gracious gift of God's Spirit.

I think here of John 3:1–8, and the famous "you must be born again/anew," or being "born of God" in 1 John 2:29 and the "washing of rebirth and renewal by the Holy Spirit" in Titus 3:5. Herein lies one of the mysteries of the gospel: in declaring the good news about Jesus, God's Spirit is at work to awaken humans to faith, and this awakening leads to a new, transformed life. This transformation process does not happen all at once,[89] but God is at work in us and through us to take what we were to become what we will be. As Dallas Willard has argued for decades, God transforms us through a vision, our intention, and the means God provides—the spiritual disciplines.[90] To create a gospel culture requires that we be converted.

But we are not alone. In fact, that previous sentence has too much of the assumption of individualism. Another way of putting it is this: the gospel is the Story of Israel that finds resolution in the saving Story of Jesus, and that story is about God's work in this world in the people of God. If we are to embrace the Gospel in order to create a gospel culture, we will also embrace the story of the Bible as a story about the people of God. We will embrace the church, warts and all, as the people of God. A gospel culture is a church culture, and it is a church culture that is being transformed—together—into a gospel culture by attending to the concerns we have expressed in the points above.

To embrace the gospel story summons us to a life of communication with God, both in listening to God and in speaking with God. We call this prayer. This is not a book about prayer, but prayer takes on two major forms: we pray spontaneously out of the depths of our heart, our wants, our desires, our hopes, and our needs. We also pray the prayers of the Bible, the psalms, and the prayers of the church, which can be found in prayer books.[91] I cannot think of prayer without thinking of the great prayer Jesus gave to us, the Lord's Prayer — and that prayer is our preeminent gospel prayer because it is shaped by Israel's Story coming to fruition in the Jesus Story. That prayer is a way of communicating with God about gospel truths.

We also embrace the gospel to create a gospel culture by *serving others in love and compassion.* Whether we look to the words of Jesus in the Jesus Creed of loving God and loving others, or to the words of Jesus in calling us to follow him, or in the words of the apostle Paul to let the Spirit of God loose in our lives to produce the fruit of the Spirit and the gifts of the Spirit, the gospel story will not leave us alone. As our God is a sending God, so we are a sent people. As our God is an other-directed God, so we are to be other-directed. The gospel propels us into mission, into the holistic mission of loving God, loving self, loving others, and loving the world.

CONCLUSION

If I am asked to break the gospel and a gospel culture down into simple statements, I would borrow imagery from the man from Northern Ireland, from Belfast, C. S. Lewis. From *The Lion, the Witch and the Wardrobe*, where we first meet the story of Aslan, we will find a few central themes about Aslan. It's the story of Aslan, which is how Lewis told the Story of Jesus:

> Watch the Lion roam.
> Watch the Lion die on the Stone Table.
> Watch the Stone Table crack with new creation powers.
> Listen to the Lion's Roar.
> Trust the Lion.
> Love the Lion.
> Live for the Lion.

There's our gospel: it's the saving Story of Israel now lived out by Jesus, who lived, died, was buried, was raised, and was exalted to God's right hand, and who is now roaring out the message that someday the kingdom will come in all its glorious fury.

Summary Statements in the New Testament

THE FOLLOWING PASSAGES complement what Paul said in 1 Corinthians 15.

Romans 1:1 – 4

Paul, a servant of Christ Jesus, called to be an apostle and set apart for the gospel of God — the gospel he promised beforehand through his prophets in the Holy Scriptures regarding his Son, who as to his earthly life was a descendant of David, and who through the Spirit of holiness was appointed the Son of God in power by his resurrection from the dead: Jesus Christ our Lord.

Romans 3:21 – 26

But now apart from the law the righteousness of God has been made known, to which the Law and the Prophets testify. This righteousness is given through faith in Jesus Christ to all who believe. There is no difference between Jew and Gentile, for all have sinned and fall short of the glory of God, and all are justified freely by his grace through the redemption that came by Christ Jesus. God presented Christ as a sacrifice of atonement, through the shedding of his blood — to be received by faith. He did this to demonstrate his righteousness, because in his forbearance he had left the sins committed beforehand unpunished — he did it to demonstrate his righteousness at the present time, so as to be just and the one who justifies those who have faith in Jesus.

PHILIPPIANS 2:5 – 11

In your relationships with one another, have the same mindset as Christ Jesus:

> Who, being in very nature God,
>> did not consider equality with God something to be used to
>>> his own advantage;
> rather, he made himself nothing
>> by taking the very nature of a servant,
>> being made in human likeness.
> And being found in *appearance as a man*,
>> he humbled himself
>> by becoming obedient to death —
>>> even death on a cross!
> Therefore God exalted him to the highest place
>> and gave him the name that is above every name,
> that at the name of Jesus every knee should bow,
>> in heaven and on earth and under the earth,
> and every tongue acknowledge that *Jesus Christ is Lord*,
> to the glory of God the Father.

COLOSSIANS 1:15 – 20

The Son is the image of the invisible God, the firstborn over all creation. For in him all things were created: things in heaven and on earth, visible and invisible, whether thrones or powers or rulers or authorities; all things have been created through him and for him. He is before all things, and in him all things hold together. And he is the head of the body, the church; he is the beginning and the firstborn from among the dead, so that in everything he might have the supremacy. For God was pleased to have all his fullness dwell in him, and through him to reconcile to himself all things, whether things on earth or things in heaven, by making peace through his blood, shed on the cross.

1 TIMOTHY 3:16

Beyond all question, the mystery from which true godliness springs
is great:

> He appeared in the flesh,
>> was vindicated by the Spirit,
> was seen by angels,
>> was preached among the nations,
> was believed on in the world,
>> was taken up in glory.

2 TIMOTHY 2:8

Remember Jesus Christ, raised from the dead, descended from
David. This is my gospel.

1 PETER 3:18 – 22

For Christ also suffered once for sins, the righteous for the unrigh-
teous, to bring you to God. He was put to death in the body but
made alive in the Spirit. After being made alive, he went and made
proclamation to the imprisoned spirits — to those who were dis-
obedient long ago when God waited patiently in the days of Noah
while the ark was being built. In it only a few people, eight in all,
were saved through water, and this water symbolizes baptism that
now saves you also — not the removal of dirt from the body but the
pledge of a clear conscience toward God. It saves you by the resurrection of Jesus Christ, who has gone into heaven and is at God's right
hand — with angels, authorities and powers in submission to him.

JUSTIN MARTYR, *FIRST APOLOGY* 66 – 67

CHAPTER 66 — OF THE EUCHARIST

And this food is called among us Eukaristia [the Eucharist], of which no one is allowed to partake but the man who believes that the things which we teach are true, and who has been washed with the washing that is for the remission of sins, and unto regeneration, and who is so living as Christ has enjoined. For not as common bread and common drink do we receive these; but in like manner as Jesus Christ our Saviour, having been made flesh by the Word of God, had both flesh and blood for our salvation, so likewise have we been taught that the food which is blessed by the prayer of His word, and from which our blood and flesh by transmutation are nourished, is the flesh and blood of that Jesus who was made flesh. For the apostles, in the memoirs composed by them, which are called Gospels, have thus delivered unto us what was enjoined upon them; that Jesus took bread, and when He had given thanks, said, "This do ye in remembrance of Me, this is My body;" and that, after the same manner, having taken the cup and given thanks, He said, "This is My blood;" and gave it to them alone. Which the wicked devils have imitated in the mysteries of Mithras, commanding the same thing to be done. For, that bread and a cup of water are placed with certain incantations in the mystic rites of one who is being initiated, you either know or can learn.

CHAPTER 67 — WEEKLY WORSHIP OF THE CHRISTIANS

And we afterwards continually remind each other of these things. And the wealthy among us help the needy; and we always keep together; and for all things wherewith we are supplied, we bless the Maker of all through His Son Jesus Christ, and through the Holy Ghost. And on the day called Sunday, all who live in cities or in the country gather together to one place, and the memoirs of the apostles or the writings of the prophets are read, as long as time permits; then, when the reader has ceased, the president verbally instructs, and exhorts to the imitation of these good things. Then we all rise together and pray, and, as we before said, when our prayer is ended, bread and wine and water are brought, and the president in like manner offers prayers and thanksgivings, according to his ability, and the people assent, saying Amen; and there is a distribution to each, and a participation of that over which thanks have been given, and to those who are absent a portion is sent by the deacons. And they who are well to do, and willing, give what each thinks fit; and what is collected is deposited with the president, who succours the orphans and widows and those who, through sickness or any other cause, are in want, and those who are in bonds and the strangers sojourning among us, and in a word takes care of all who are in need. But Sunday is the day on which we all hold our common assembly, because it is the first day on which God, having wrought a change in the darkness and matter, made the world; and Jesus Christ our Saviour on the same day rose from the dead. For He was crucified on the day before that of Saturn (Saturday); and on the day after that of Saturn, which is the day of the Sun, having appeared to His apostles and disciples, He taught them these things, which we have submitted to you also for your consideration.[92]

SERMONS IN ACTS

PETER'S GOSPEL SERMON ON PENTECOST (ACTS 2:14 – 39)

Then Peter stood up with the Eleven, raised his voice and addressed the crowd: "Fellow Jews and all of you who live in Jerusalem, let me explain this to you; listen carefully to what I say. These people are not drunk, as you suppose. It's only nine in the morning!" (vv. 14 – 15)

Notice how Peter moves immediately to the Old Testament story to explain what is happening with Jesus and his followers:

"No, this is what was spoken by the prophet Joel:
" 'In the last days, God says,
   I will pour out my Spirit on all people.
Your sons and daughters will prophesy,
   your young men will see visions,
   your old men will dream dreams.
Even on my servants, both men and women,
   I will pour out my Spirit in those days,
   and they will prophesy.
I will show wonders in the heavens above
   and signs on the earth below,
   blood and fire and billows of smoke.
The sun will be turned to darkness

and the moon to blood
before the coming of the great and glorious day of the Lord.
And everyone who calls
on the name of the Lord will be saved.'" (vv. 16–21)

He tells the Story about Jesus: life, death, resurrection, exaltation.

"Fellow Israelites, listen to this: Jesus of Nazareth was a man accredited by God to you by miracles, wonders and signs, which God did among you through him, as you yourselves know. This man was handed over to you by God's deliberate plan and foreknowledge; and you, with the help of wicked men put him to death by nailing him to the cross. But God raised him from the dead, freeing him from the agony of death, because it was impossible for death to keep its hold on him. (vv. 22–24)

Jesus, the Davidic messianic King, is foretold in Israel's Story

"David said about him:
"'I saw the Lord always before me.
    Because he is at my right hand,
    I will not be shaken.
Therefore my heart is glad and my tongue rejoices;
    my body also will rest in hope,
because you will not abandon me to the realm of the dead,
    you will not let your holy one see decay.
You have made known to me the paths of life;
    you will fill me with joy in your presence.'

"Fellow Israelites, I can tell you confidently that the patriarch David died and was buried, and his tomb is here to this day. But he was a prophet and knew that God had promised him on oath that he would place one of his descendants on his throne. Seeing what was to come, he spoke of the resurrection of the Messiah, that he was not abandoned to the realm of the dead, nor did his body see decay." (vv. 25–31)

Dead, raised, and exalted as King

"God has raised this Jesus to life, and we are all witnesses of it. Exalted to the right hand of God, he has received from the Father the promised Holy Spirit and has poured out what you now see and hear." (vv. 32–33)

Israel's Story once again

"For David did not ascend to heaven, and yet he said,
" 'The Lord said to my Lord:
    "Sit at my right hand
until I make your enemies
    a footstool for your feet." ' " (vv. 34–35)

The point of the gospel!

"Therefore let all Israel be assured of this: God has made this Jesus, whom you crucified, both Lord and Messiah." (v. 36)

How to respond to the apostolic gospel of Peter

When the people heard this, they were cut to the heart and said to Peter and the other apostles, "Brothers, what shall we do?"

Peter replied, "Repent and be baptized, every one of you, in the name of Jesus Christ ..." (vv. 37–38a)

Saving benefits for responders

... for the forgiveness of your sins. And you will receive the gift of the Holy Spirit. The promise is for you and your children and for all who are far off—for all whom the Lord our God will call." (vv. 38b–39)

PETER'S SECOND GOSPEL SERMON IN ACTS (ACTS 3:12 – 26)

When Peter saw this, he said to them: "Fellow Israelites, why does this surprise you? Why do you stare at us as if by our own power or godliness we had made this man walk? (v. 12)

Peter goes to Israel's Story to explain a healing—he appeals to the God who raised Jesus from the dead and tells the gospel story

"The God of Abraham, Isaac and Jacob, the God of our fathers, has glorified his servant Jesus. You handed him over to be killed, and you disowned him before Pilate, though he had decided to let him go. You disowned the Holy and Righteous One and asked that a murderer be released to you. You killed the author of life, but God raised him from the dead. We are witnesses of this." (vv. 13–15)

Faith in the raised-from-the-dead Jesus heals

"By faith in the name of Jesus, this man whom you see and know was made strong. It is Jesus' name and the faith that comes through him that has completely healed him, as you can all see." (v. 16)

Back to Israel's Story to explain Jesus' suffering

"Now, fellow Israelites, I know that you acted in ignorance, as did your leaders. But this is how God fulfilled what he had foretold through all the prophets, saying that his Messiah would suffer." (vv. 17–18)

How to respond to the gospel

"Repent, then, and turn to God ..." (v 19a)

Saving benefits for responders

"... so that your sins may be wiped out, that times of refreshing may come from the Lord, and that he may send the Messiah, who has been appointed for you—even Jesus." (vv. 19b–20)

Back to Israel's Story again: second coming, Gentile inclusion

"Heaven must receive him until the time comes for God to restore everything, as he promised long ago through his holy prophets. For Moses said, 'The Lord your God will raise up for you a prophet like me from among your own people; you must listen to everything he tells you. Anyone who does not listen to him will be completely cut off from their people.'

"Indeed, beginning with Samuel, all the prophets who have spoken have foretold these days. And you are heirs of the prophets and of the covenant God made with your fathers. He said to Abraham, 'Through your offspring all peoples on earth will be blessed.' When God raised up his servant, he sent him first to you to bless you by turning each of you from your wicked ways." (vv. 21–26)

A SUMMARY OF PETER'S GOSPEL PREACHING (ACTS 4:8 – 12)

Main themes: gospel story of Jesus, Israel's Story is the framing story

Then Peter, filled with the Holy Spirit, said to them: "Rulers and elders of the people! If we are being called to account today for an act of kindness shown to a man who was lame and are being asked how he was healed, then know this, you and all the people of Israel: It is by the name of Jesus Christ of Nazareth, whom you crucified but whom God raised from the dead, that this man stands before you healed. Jesus is

" 'the stone you builders rejected,
   which has become the cornerstone.'

Salvation is found in no one else, for there is no other name under heaven given to mankind by which we must be saved."

PETER'S FAMOUS CORNELIUS SERMON: GOSPEL FOR GENTILES (ACTS 10:34 – 43)
Themes: Story of Jesus is sketched—framework for Gospels

Then Peter began to speak: "I now realize how true it is that God does not show favoritism but accepts from every nation the one who fears him and does what is right. You know the message God sent to the people of Israel, announcing the good news of peace through Jesus Christ, who is Lord of all. You know what has happened throughout the province of Judea, beginning in Galilee after the baptism that John preached—how God anointed Jesus of Nazareth with the Holy Spirit and power, and how he went around doing good and healing all who were under the power of the devil, because God was with him.

"We are witnesses of everything he did in the country of the Jews and in Jerusalem. They killed him by hanging him on a cross, but God raised him from the dead on the third day and caused him to be seen. He was not seen by all the people, but by witnesses whom God had already chosen—by us who ate and drank with him after he rose from the dead." (vv. 34–41)

Includes his exaltation as judge

"He commanded us to preach to the people and to testify that he is the one whom God appointed as judge of the living and the dead." (v. 42)

Israel's Story and saving benefits

"All the prophets testify about him that everyone who believes in him receives forgiveness of sins through his name." (v. 43)

PETER'S TESTIMONY OF GOD'S WORK AMONG GENTILES THROUGH HIS GOSPELING (ACTS 11:4 – 18)

Peter told them the whole story: "I was in the city of Joppa praying, and in a trance I saw a vision. I saw something like a large sheet being let down from heaven by its four corners, and it came down to where I was. I looked into it and saw four-footed animals of the earth, wild beasts, reptiles and birds. Then I heard a voice telling me, 'Get up, Peter. Kill and eat.'

"I replied, 'Surely not, Lord! Nothing impure or unclean has ever entered my mouth.'

"The voice spoke from heaven a second time, 'Do not call anything impure that God has made clean.' This happened three times, and then it was all pulled up to heaven again.

"Right then three men who had been sent to me from Caesarea stopped at the house where I was staying. The Spirit told me to have no hesitation about going with them. These six brothers also went with me, and we entered the man's house. He told us how he had seen an angel appear in his house and say, 'Send to Joppa for Simon who is called Peter. He will bring you a message through which you and all your household will be saved.'

"As I began to speak, the Holy Spirit came on them as he had come on us at the beginning. Then I remembered what the Lord had said: 'John baptized with water, but you will be baptized with the Holy Spirit.' So if God gave them the same gift he gave us who believed in the Lord Jesus Christ, who was I to think that I could stand in God's way?"

When they heard this, they had no further objections and praised God, saying, "So then, even to Gentiles God has granted repentance that leads to life."

PAUL'S GOSPELING IN ANTIOCH (ACTS 13:16 – 41)

Standing up, Paul motioned with his hand and said: "Fellow Israelites and you Gentiles who worship God, listen to me!" (v. 16)

Where to begin? With Israel's Story

"The God of the people of Israel chose our ancestors; he made the people prosper during their stay in Egypt; with mighty power he led them out of that country; for about forty years he endured their conduct in the wilderness; and he overthrew seven nations in Canaan, giving their land to his people as their inheritance. All this took about 450 years.

"After this, God gave them judges until the time of Samuel the prophet. Then the people asked for a king, and he gave them Saul son of Kish, of the tribe of Benjamin, who ruled forty years. After removing Saul, he made David their king. God testified concerning him: 'I have found David son of Jesse, a man after my own heart; he will do everything I want him to do.'" (vv. 17–22)

The Story leads to the Story of Jesus, with John as one who pointed to Jesus

"From this man's descendants God has brought to Israel the Savior Jesus, as he promised. Before the coming of Jesus, John preached repentance and baptism to all the people of Israel. As John was completing his work, he said: 'Who do you suppose I am? I am not the one you are looking for. But there is one coming after me whose sandals I am not worthy to untie.'" (vv. 23–25)

The saving Story of Jesus: life, death. and resurrection

"Fellow children of Abraham and you God-fearing Gentiles, it is to us that this message of salvation has been sent. The people of Jerusalem and their rulers did not recognize Jesus, yet in condemning him they fulfilled the words of the prophets that are read every Sabbath. Though they found no proper ground for a death sentence, they asked Pilate to have him executed. When they had carried out all that was written about him, they took him down from the cross and laid him in a tomb. But God raised him from the dead, and for many days he was seen by those who had traveled with him from Galilee to Jerusalem. They are now his witnesses to our people." (vv. 26–31)

Back to Israel's Story as promising the King Jesus gospel

"We tell you the good news: What God promised our ancestors he has fulfilled for us, their children, by raising up Jesus. As it is written in the second Psalm:

" 'You are my son;
today I have become your father.'

God raised him from the dead so that he will never be subject to decay. As God has said,

" 'I will give you the holy and sure blessings promised to David.'

So it is also stated elsewhere:

" 'You will not let your holy one see decay.'

"Now when David had served God's purpose in his own generation, he fell asleep; he was buried with his ancestors and his body decayed. But the one whom God raised from the dead did not see decay." (vv. 32–37)

How to respond, saving benefits

"Therefore, my friends, I want you to know that through Jesus the forgiveness of sins is proclaimed to you. Through him everyone who believes is set free from every sin, a justification you were not able to obtain under the law of Moses." (vv. 38–39)

One more time, back to Israel's Story

"Take care that what the prophets have said does not happen to you:
" 'Look, you scoffers,
wonder and perish,
for I am going to do something in your days
that you would never believe,
even if someone told you.' " (vv. 40–41)

SUMMARY OF A GOSPEL SERMON OF PAUL'S IN LYSTRA (ACTS 14:15–17)
Themes: repent, God is Creator, natural revelation

"Friends, why are you doing this? We too are only human, like you. We are bringing you good news, telling you to turn from these worthless things to the living God, who made the heavens and the earth and the sea and everything in them. In the past, he let all nations go their own way. Yet he has not left himself without testimony: He has shown kindness by giving you rain from heaven and crops in their seasons; he provides you with plenty of food and fills your hearts with joy."

PAUL'S FAMOUS AREOPAGUS SERMON (ACTS 17:22 – 31)

Touchstone: worship of God, God yearning

Paul then stood up in the meeting of the Areopagus and said: "People of Athens! I see that in every way you are very religious. For as I walked around and looked carefully at your objects of worship, I even found an altar with this inscription: TO AN UNKNOWN GOD. So you are ignorant of the very thing you worship—and this is what I am going to proclaim to you." (vv. 22–23)

Story of Israel as universal human story

"The God who made the world and everything in it is the Lord of heaven and earth and does not live in temples built by human hands. And he is not served by human hands, as if he needed anything. Rather, he himself gives everyone life and breath and everything else." (vv. 24–25)

Slips in Adam as the "one man"

"From one man he made all the nations, that they should inhabit the whole earth; and he marked out their appointed times in history and the boundaries of their lands. God did this so that they would seek him and perhaps reach out for him and find him, though he is not far from any one of us. 'For in him we live and move and have our being.' As some of your own poets have said, 'We are his offspring.'

"Therefore since we are God's offspring, we should not think that the divine being is like gold or silver or stone—an image made by human design and skill." (vv. 26–29)

How to respond: repent in light of judgment by Jesus

"In the past God overlooked such ignorance, but now he commands all people everywhere to repent. For he has set a day when he will judge the world with justice by the man he has appointed." (vv. 30–31a)

Resurrection of Jesus as apologetic reason to listen

"He has given proof of this to everyone by raising him from the dead." (v. 31b)

AFTER WORDS

THIS BOOK IS THE RESULT of years of Bible reading and prayer, teaching and preaching, and lecturing in colleges, seminaries, and conferences. In the opening pages to this book I paid tribute to those who have invited me to lecture, and it would be fun to write out stories about each place, but those indulgences will be have to be done in person. But I want to thank again the many friends and colleagues who have been part of this project, including Attie Nel, Marius Nel, Coenie Burger, Theo Geyser, David deSilva, John Byron, Allan Bevere, Wes Olmstead, Patrick Mitchel (whose name represents the many fine leaders at Irish Bible Institute); Jerry Rushford, Chuck Conniry, Terry Dawson; *Leadership* magazine's Marshall Shelley and Skye Jethani, who provoked me to write something on gospeling for iGens; George Kalantzis, who invited me to address a group of patristic scholars on the gospel; Gerald McDermott, who invited me to write something on evangelicalism's gospel theology; Kevin Corcoran, for the invitation to write about the gospel and atonement in the book of Acts; and Mark Galli and the folks at *Christianity Today* for publishing a sketch of some themes in this book.

To my Fourth-Year Seminar students in the fall of 2010 I owe the debt of listening to this book and interacting with it. Their class presentations on theologians, from Pope Benedict to Henri Lubac to Athanasius to Rob Bell to Anne Carr and to John Piper, stimulated my thinking and in one way or another have impacted this book. A former graduate assistant, Chris Ridgeway, and his paper "Napkin Evangelism: The Evangelical Rhetoric of Conversion in Gospel Diagrams Old and New," gave me all kinds of suggestions of how to frame what I call here "salvation culture."

My colleagues at North Park University, Greg Clark, Brad Nassif, Joel Willitts, Mary Veeneman, and Boaz Johnson, are a source of friendship but also have answered offhand questions about gospel concerns, and I record again my debt to David Parkyn and North Park University for providing me with such a wonderful setting to teach and write. Roseanne Sension, a friend, read the manuscript, asked some questions, and made the book better, as did also Mike Bird, J. Daniel Kirk, and David Fitch.

My literary agent, Greg Daniel, supports and mentors my books in ways that exceed expectations. One of his suggestions led to much greater clarity in the latter half of this book. Thanks also to John Raymond, my friend and editor at Zondervan, for his support of this project as well as his judicious suggestions on how to make this book more readable. Verlyn Verbrugge, another editor at Zondervan, brought the book through the publishing process.

No words can adequately express my love and gratitude to Kris. After two longs days in Stellenbosch, South Africa, of hearing various lecturers on the book of Acts, including mine on the gospel in Acts, Kris said, "Your paper was the best one." After two long days of my giving lectures on the gospel in Dublin, Ireland, as we were returning to our room, Kris said, "That got long." Here, my dear, is the end of it. (You hope.)

Christmas Eve Day 2010

NOTES

1. C. H. Dodd, *The Apostolic Preaching and Its Developments* (New York: Harper and Row, 1964), 76.
2. N. T. Wright, *What Saint Paul Really Said: Was Paul of Tarsus the Real Founder of Christianity?* (Grand Rapids: Eerdmans, 1997), 41.
3. The sidebar comments come from students of mine. Names have been changed, but the students have given me permission to use their words.
4. See the report at http://ns.umich.edu/htdocs/releases/story.php?id=8155, which approaches church attendance from the angle of whether American Christians tell the truth about going to church.
5. This is from personal correspondence and communication with David Kinnaman; the statistics he sent me were dated December 17, 2010.
6. On this, see Kenda Creasy Dean, *Almost Christian: What the Faith of American Teenagers Is Telling the American Church* (New York: Oxford, 2010).
7. Defining "evangelical" has its own history of debate, and I side with Mark Noll and David Bebbington. An excellent version of this can now be found in Timothy Larsen, "Defining and Locating Evangelicalism," in *The Cambridge Companion to Evangelical Theology* (ed. T. Larsen and D. J. Treier; Cambridge: Cambridge Univ. Press, 2007), 1, who finds five factors. In brief, an evangelical is an orthodox Protestant who is part of a global network that arose out of the eighteenth-century revivals, who gives the Bible a preeminent place in matters of faith and practice, who stresses reconciliation with God through the atoning work on the cross, and who stresses as well the work of the Holy Spirit to convert, restore, empower, and compel into mission. See also M. Noll, "What Is an Evangelical?" in *The Oxford Handbook of Evangelical Theology* (ed. G. R. McDermott; New York: Oxford Univ. Press, 2010), 19–32.
8. Frank O'Connor, *An Only Child* (New York: Knopf, 1961), 37.
9. See *The Apostolic Fathers* (ed. M. W. Holmes; Grand Rapids: Baker, 2007), 694–719.
10. See J. H. Leith, *Creeds of the Churches* (rev. ed.; Atlanta: John Knox, 1977), 239–51.
11. See *John Wesley's Sermons: An Anthology* (ed. A. C. Outler and R. P. Heitzenrater; Nashville: Abingdon, 1987), e.g., 335–45, 371–80, 381–91.

12. Alongside that original apostolic gospel tradition the early church sometimes also summed up what they believed in other short confessional statements, and I have listed a few of these in Appendix 1 at the end of this book.

13. What brought this to the fore was Richard Hays, *Echoes of Scripture in the Letters of Paul* (New Haven, CT: Yale Univ. Press, 1989); *The Conversion of Imagination: Paul as Interpreter of Israel's Scriptures* (Grand Rapids: Eerdmans, 2005).

14. Darrell Bock, *Recovering the Real Lost Gospel* (Nashville: Broadman and Holman, 2010), 7–21.

15. Brenda Colijn, *Images of Salvation in the New Testament* (Downers Grove, IL: InterVarsity Press, 2010).

16. See my *A Community Called Atonement* (Nashville: Abingdon, 2007).

17. Colijn, *Images of Salvation*, 314.

18. The Eastern Church has explored this more than any other tradition. I recommend the exceptional sketch of the issues and texts in Archbishop Hilarion Alfeyev, *Christ the Conqueror of Hell: The Descent into Hades from an Orthodox Perspective* (Crestwood, NY: St. Vladimir's Seminary Press, 2009).

19. I am tempted here to engage in pages of exposition of the eschatological reality, the now but not yet, that shapes so much of the gospel. Alas, I shall indulge only a few things to read: from G. E. Ladd, *A Theology of the New Testament* (rev. ed.; D. A. Hagner, ed.; Grand Rapids: Eerdmans, 1993) to J. Moltmann, *A Theology of Hope* (New York: Harper and Row, 1965), and *The Coming of God* (Minneapolis: Fortress, 2004).

20. All quotations are from N. T. Wright, *What Saint Paul Really Said*, 39–62.

21. For many *ordo salutis* will mean the particular order of events in the saving process, and a definitive Reformed statement is J. Murray, *Redemption: Accomplished and Applied* (Grand Rapids: Eerdmans, 1955), where the order is effectual calling, regeneration, faith/repentance, justification, adoption, sanctification, perseverance, union with Christ, and glorification.

22. Greg Gilbert, *What Is the Gospel?* (Wheaton, IL: Crossway, 2010), and I focus here on pp. 27–36. The criticisms in the next paragraph come from throughout the book.

23. There are no italics anywhere in the NIV text, so all italics in quotes from the NIV have been added to the text to draw attention to certain elements.

24. An excellent study of Paul's use of shorthand is Margaret M. Mitchell, "Rhetorical Shorthand in Pauline Argumentation: The Functions of 'The Gospel' in the Corinthian Correspondence," in *Gospel in Paul: Studies on Corinthians, Galatians and Romans for Richard N. Longenecker* (ed. L. Ann Jervis and Peter Richardson; Sheffield: Sheffield Academic Press, 1994), 63–88.

25. Ted Campbell, *The Gospel in Christian Traditions* (New York: Oxford, 2009).

26. Jaroslav Pelikan, *Credo: Historical and Theological Guide to Creeds and Confessions of Faith in the Christian Tradition* (New Haven, CT: Yale Univ. Press, 2003).

27. Somewhere around AD 110.

28. On Ignatius, see C. T. Brown, *The Gospel and Ignatius of Antioch* (New York: Peter Lang, 2000).

29. Irenaeus, *Against Heresies* 1.10.1.

30. Tertullian, *Against Praxeas* 2. See also his *On the Veiling of Virgins* 1.

31. There is serious dispute on the origins and authorship of *The Apostolic Tradition*; for full discussion, see P. F. Bradshaw, M. E. Johnson, and L. E. Phillips, *The Apostolic Tradition* (Hermeneia; Minneapolis: Fortress, 2002).

32. Hippolytus, *The Apostolic Tradition* 21.

33. See Justin Martyr, *First Apology* 61, and *The Epistula Apostolorum*, and the story-shaped approach in Irenaeus, *The Demonstration of the Apostolic Teaching* 3, which frames the gospel in light of 1 Corinthians 15's set of facts. See also his *Against Heresies* 1.49.

34. See Lewis Ayres, *Nicaea and Its Legacy: An Approach to Fourth-Century Trinitarian Theology* (Oxford: Oxford Univ. Press, 2006).

35. Found at the end of the NT ms Codex E; in Ambrose; in Sermons 213, 215 by Augustine; in Sermons 57–62 by Peter Chrysologus, bishop of Ravenna (400–450); and then completely in Rufinus of Aquileia's commentary on it (c. 404). From L. T. Johnson, *The Creed: What Christians Believe and Why it Matters* (New York: Doubleday, 2003), 31.

36. For two excellent studies of the conversion experience, see P. Caldwell, *The Puritan Conversion Narrative: The Beginnings of American Expression* (Cambridge: Cambridge Univ. Press, 1983); D. Bruce Hindmarsh, *The Evangelical Conversion Narrative: Spiritual Autobiography in Early Modern England* (Oxford: Oxford Univ. Press, 2005). A point deserves to be made: evangelicalism can be broadly defined as the Protestant Reformation churches or those who are faithful to the Reformation, or it can be defined more narrowly as a movement of the post-Reformation churches that began in the eighteenth century. For the sake of simplification, I'm using it in the broader sense here because many of those who equate "gospel" with "plan of salvation" define evangelicalism in that broader sense.

37. John Wesley, "I Felt My Heart Strangely Warmed," www.ccel.org/ccel/wesley/journal.vi.ii.xvi.html (accessed July 7, 2010).

38. Dallas Willard, *The Divine Conspiracy: Rediscovering Our Hidden Life in God* (San Francisco: HarperSanFrancisco, 1998), 35–59.

39. This is from ibid., 403, n. 8, and is perhaps one of the most frequently quoted footnotes in history!

40. John Dickson, *The Best Kept Secret of Christian Mission: Promoting the Gospel with More Than Our Lips* (Grand Rapids: Zondervan, 2010); all quotations are from pp. 111–40.

41. F. F. Bruce, *The Defense of the Gospel in the New Testament* (Grand Rapids: Eerdmans, 1977), 4. For a full study of this, see M. Hengel, *The Four Gospels*

and the One Gospel of Jesus Christ (trans. J. Bowden; Harrisburg, PA: Trinity Press International, 2000), 34 – 115.

42. Augustine, *Tractates on the Gospel according to St. John* 36.1.

43. Dickson, *Best Kept Secret*, 140.

44. Joseph Cardinal Ratzinger [Pope Benedict XVI], *Gospel, Catechesis, Catechism: Sidelights on the* Catechism of the Catholic Church (San Francisco: Ignatius, 1997), 51.

45. Hengel, *Four Gospels and the One Gospel of Jesus Christ*, 91.

46. I. H. Marshall, "Luke and His 'Gospel,'" in *The Gospel and the Gospels* (ed. P. Stuhlmacher; Grand Rapids: Eerdmans, 1991), 273 – 92, quoting from p. 283.

47. Mark's gospel ends abruptly and oddly and ungospel-like at 16:8 with "for they were afraid," and many today think the last page of Mark's gospel has been lost. Anyone can consult the last page of Mark in a Bible and read the textual notes and see that there are two endings, one shorter and one longer, and neither of them is the original ending. The original ending, again, seems to have been lost and to compensate for it, some early Christians filled in the gap! For a good discussion, see R. T. France, *The Gospel of Mark* (Grand Rapids: Eerdmans, 2002), 670 – 74, 685 – 88.

48. I draw attention again to Darrell Bock's book *Recovering the Real Lost Gospel* as an excellent example of how the Old Testament — story and promises and expectations — shapes the early Christian understanding of the gospel, and I draw your attention away from the sadly true but many, many examples of "gospel" that don't even need an Old Testament.

49. See, e.g., R. E. Brown, *The Gospel according to John (I-XII)* (AB 29; Garden City, NY: Doubleday, 1966), 205 – 415.

50. R. N. Longenecker, *Biblical Exegesis in the Apostolic Period* (Grand Rapids: Eerdmans, 1975), 153 (see pp. 152 – 57).

51. An older technical book on this is still of much value: G. N. Stanton, *Jesus of Nazareth in New Testament Preaching* (Cambridge: Cambridge Univ. Press, 1977).

52. Eusebius, *Church History* 3.39.14 – 16.

53. John Piper, *God Is the Gospel* (Wheaton, IL: Crossway, 2005), 13.

54. Most likely Jacob-Israel, who did not complete his task and wherein is surely a tensive symbol rather than simply a cryptic identifier. For a recent sketch of the options, see J. Goldingay, *The Message of Isaiah 40 – 55: A Literary-Theological Commentary* (London: T&T Clark, 2005), 150 – 54.

55. See Origen, *Commentary on Matthew* 14.7. Thus, in Greek, Jesus is *autosophia, autodikaiôsynç, autoalçtheia,* and *autobasileia.*

56. There is scholarly debate about this text. I agree with this dimension of the fascinating study of J. A. T. Robinson, *Twelve New Testament Studies* (London: SCM, 1984), 28 – 52.

57. For the Dead Sea Scrolls, see Florentino García Martínez, *The Dead Sea Scrolls Translated* (Grand Rapids: Eerdmans, 1996).

58. Rudolf Bultmann, *Theology of the New Testament* (2 vols; New York: Charles Scribner's, 1955), 1:33.

59. This paragraph is indebted to my study "Jesus and the Twelve," in D. L. Bock and R. L. Webb, eds., *Key Events in the Life of the Historical Jesus: A Collaborative Exploration of Context and Coherence* (WUNT 247; Tübingen: Mohr Siebeck, 2009), 181–214.

60. Scot McKnight, *Jesus and His Death: Historiography, the Historical Jesus, and Atonement Theory* (Waco, TX: Baylor Univ. Press, 2005).

61. K. Snodgrass, "The Gospel of Jesus," in *The Written Gospel* (ed. M. Bockmuehl and D. A. Hagner; Cambridge: Cambridge Univ. Press, 2005), 31–44, here p. 43.

62. Joseph Cardinal Ratzinger [Pope Benedict XVI], *Gospel, Catechesis, Catechism* (San Francisco: Ignatius Press, 1977), 52.

63. J. D. G. Dunn, *The Acts of the Apostles* (Valley Forge, PA: Trinity Press International, 1996), 177. Let me justify his point: The basics are the same: we find the Story of Israel coming to a climax and fulfillment in the Story of Jesus (Acts 13:17–22, 32–37). We find a similar focus on the death of Jesus as an act of injustice, with Paul shifting blame slightly toward the people (13:27–28). We also find in Paul's gospeling a focus on the resurrection as an act of God's vindication of Jesus (13:30–31, 32–37). And this gospeling of Paul leads to, or is rooted in, a *Christology* in which the vindicated Jesus is seen as the Davidic Savior (13:23, 33–37). And, Paul's gospeling leads to a summons to repent (13:40–41) for the forgiveness of sins (13:38–39; cf. 17:30). In the two major gospelings of Paul in Acts (13:16–41 and 17:22–31), we do not hear tones of the exaltation of Christ to the right hand of God, and we hear nothing of the gift of the Holy Spirit. But one would be hard-pressed to deny that Paul's gospel is much the same as Peter's. That both refer to Psalm 16:10 notably connects the two apostles (cf. Acts 2:25–28; 13:35).

64. Perhaps Peter unwittingly anticipates the Gentile mission in these words because he won't—and then not with enthusiasm—extend the gospel to Gentiles for seven more chapters. In Galatians Paul will make use of this blessing for the nations verse, and one has to wonder if he picked this up in part from the gospel sermons of Peter. (Paul suggests in Galatians 1 that he didn't get the idea from Peter.)

65. The expression comes from Richard Hays, *The Conversion of the Imagination* (Grand Rapids: Eerdmans, 2005).

66. Thus, his life (2:22; 10:37–38; cf. 11:16), his death (2:23; 3:13–14; 10:39), his resurrection (2:24–32; 3:15; 10:40–42), his exaltation (2:33), the gift of the Holy Spirit (2:33–35), and his second coming as judge (3:20; 10:42).

67. Fleming Rutledge, *Not Ashamed of the Gospel* (Grand Rapids: Eerdmans, 2007), 157–63.

68. Again, I point your attention to Darrell Bock, *Recovering the Real Lost Gospel.*.

69. Many connect Paul's words here to 1 Thessalonians 1:9–10, where Paul sums

up what must have been a common conversion from idolatries, that the people of those regions "report what kind of reception you gave us. They tell how you turned to God from idols to serve the living and true God, and to wait for his Son from heaven, whom he raised from the dead—Jesus, who rescues us from the coming wrath."

70. N. T. Wright, *The Resurrection of the Son of God* (Minneapolis: Fortress, 2003).
71. On baptism, see now E. Ferguson, *Baptism in the Early Church: History, Theology, and Liturgy in the First Five Centuries* (Grand Rapids: Eerdmans, 2009), esp. 166–85.
72. This is emphatic in the gospel of John, where the verb "to believe" (*pisteuō*) in its various forms appears nearly one hundred times and refers to one's trust, one's abiding, one's obedience, one's commitment, and one's drawing of life itself from union with Christ.
73. Neither at Pisidian Antioch nor on the Areopagus does Paul call his audience to baptism. Paul himself was baptized (cf. Acts 9:18; 22:16), and in other settings baptism followed response to the gospel (16:15, 33; 18:8; 19:3–5). But it is a strange curiosity that Paul does not demand baptism in his gospeling sermons. Maybe it was assumed by Luke to be so obvious it didn't need to be mentioned, but making assumptions about what to us is so obvious is the way we got ourselves into the "gospel" mess that concerns this book!
74. This point has been made many times, but one exceptional example is from an old book by A. M. Hunter, *The Unity of the New Testament* (London: SCM, 1943), 20–33.
75. W. H. Kimnach, K. P. Minkema, and D. A. Sweeney, *The Sermons of Jonathan Edwards: A Reader* (New Haven, CT: Yale Univ. Press, 1999), 49–65. His sermon "Heaven Is a World of Love" can be found at pp. 242–72.
76. John Walton, *The Lost World of Genesis One: Ancient Cosmology and the Origins Debate* (Downers Grove, IL: InterVarsity Press, 2009).
77. G. N. Stanton, *Jesus of Nazareth in New Testament Preaching* (Cambridge: Cambridge Univ. Press, 1977), 24–25. For a more balanced approach, see W. Horbury, "'Gospel' in Herodian Judaea," in *The Written Gospel* (ed. M. Bockmuehl and D. A. Hagner; Cambridge: Cambridge Univ. Press, 2007), 7–30, and J. D. G. Dunn, *The Theology of Paul the Apostle* (Grand Rapids: Eerdmans, 1998), 164–69.
78. M. Bird, *Introducing Paul: The Man, His Mission and His Message* (Downers Grove, IL: InterVarsity Press, 2008), 88.
79. See the balanced study of C. Kavin Rowe, *World Upside Down: Reading Acts in the Graeco-Roman Age* (Oxford: Oxford Univ. Press, 2009).
80. Dallas Willard, *The Divine Conspiracy: Rediscovering Our Hidden Life in God* (San Francisco: HarperSanFrancisco, 1998), 35–59.
81. I've heard this story a few times, the most recent of which was from David Fitch.
82. Sean Gladding, *The Story of God, The Story of Us: Getting Lost and Found in the Bible* (Downers Grove, IL: InterVarsity Press, 2010).

83. Here see R. E. Webber, *Ancient-Future Time: Forming Spirituality through the Christian Year* (Grand Rapids: Baker, 2004).

84. Scot McKnight, *One.Life: Jesus Calls, We Follow* (Grand Rapids: Zondervan, 2010).

85. Gabe Lyons, *The Next Christians: The Good News about the End of Christian America* (New York: Doubleday, 2010).

86. Justo Gonzalez, *The Story of Christianity* (2 volumes; San Francisco: Harper-One, 2010).

87. Chris Armstrong, *Patron Saints for Postmoderns* (Downers Grove, IL: InterVarsity Press, 2009).

88. Steve Wilkens and Mark L. Sanford, *Hidden Worldviews: Eight Cultural Stories That Shape Our Lives* (Downers Grove, IL: InterVarsity Press, 2009).

89. See my book *Turning to Jesus* (Louisville: Westminster John Knox, 2002).

90. Dallas Willard, *Renovation of the Heart* (Colorado Springs: NavPress, 2002).

91. I introduce prayer books in *Praying with the Church* (Brewster, MA: Paraclete, 2006).

92. See www.earlychristianwritings.com/text/justinmartyr-firstapology.html.

One.Life

Jesus Calls, We Follow

Scot McKnight, author of
The Jesus Creed

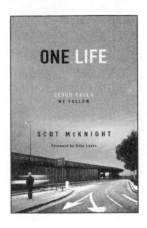

What is the "Christian life" all about?

Studying the Bible, attending church, cultivating a prayer life, witnessing to others—those are all good. But is that really what Jesus has in mind?

The answer, says Scot McKnight in *One.Life*, lies in Jesus' words, "Follow me."

What does it look like to follow Jesus, and how will doing so change the way we live our life—our love.life, our justice.life, our peace.life, our community.life, our sex.life—everything about our life?

One.Life will open your eyes to the full, compelling immensity of what it means to be a Christian. "Jesus offers to us a kingdom dream that transforms us to the very core of our being," says Scot McKnight. "His vision is so big we are called to give our entire life to it. His vision is so big it swallows up our dreams."

Discover exactly what Jesus meant when he announced the arrival of God's kingdom. Equipping you with a new understanding of that kingdom's radical nature, *One.Life* shares profound, challenging, and practical insights on how to demonstrate its reality in your life.

In many ways, what *The Cost of Discipleship* by Dietrich Bonhoeffer challenged Christians to do in earlier generations, *One.Life* will do for a new generation.

One.Life will call you beyond the flatlands of religiosity toward a kingdom vision that will shape everything you do.

Available in stores and online!

The Blue Parakeet

Rethinking How You Read the Bible

Scot McKnight, Author of
The Jesus Creed

Why can't I just be a Christian?"

Parakeets make delightful pets. We cage them or clip their wings to keep them where we want them. Scot McKnight contends that many, conservatives and liberals alike, attempt the same thing with the Bible. We all try to tame it.

McKnight's *The Blue Parakeet* has emerged at the perfect time to cool the flames of a world on fire with contention and controversy. It calls Christians to a way to read the Bible that leads beyond old debates and denominational battles. It calls Christians to stop taming the Bible and to let it speak anew for a new generation.

In his books *The Jesus Creed and Embracing Grace*, Scot McKnight established himself as one of America's finest Christian thinkers. In *The Blue Parakeet*, McKnight touches the hearts and minds of today's Christians, challenging them to rethink how to read the Bible—not just to puzzle it together into some systematic theology but to see it as a Story that we're summoned to enter and to carry forward in our day.

In his own inimitable style, McKnight sets traditional and liberal Christianity on its ear, leaving readers equipped, encouraged, and emboldened to be the people of faith they long to be.

Share Your Thoughts

With the Author: Your comments will be forwarded to the author when you send them to *zauthor@zondervan.com*.

With Zondervan: Submit your review of this book by writing to *zreview@zondervan.com*.

Free Online Resources at
www.zondervan.com

Zondervan AuthorTracker: Be notified whenever your favorite authors publish new books, go on tour, or post an update about what's happening in their lives at www.zondervan.com/authortracker.

Daily Bible Verses and Devotions: Enrich your life with daily Bible verses or devotions that help you start every morning focused on God. Visit www.zondervan.com/newsletters.

Free Email Publications: Sign up for newsletters on Christian living, academic resources, church ministry, fiction, children's resources, and more. Visit www.zondervan.com/newsletters.

Zondervan Bible Search: Find and compare Bible passages in a variety of translations at www.zondervanbiblesearch.com.

Other Benefits: Register yourself to receive online benefits like coupons and special offers, or to participate in research.

ZONDERVAN.com/
AUTHORTRACKER
follow your favorite authors